HOW TO PIONEER

(even if you haven't a clue)

David Male

CHURCH HOUSE
PUBLISHING

Church House Publishing
Church House
Great Smith Street
London SW1P 3AZ

ISBN 978 1 78140 001 2

Published 2016 by Church House Publishing
Copyright © David Male 2016

Second impression 2017

The opinions expressed in this book are those of the author
and do not necessarily reflect the official policy of the General
Synod or The Archbishops' Council of the Church of England.

Scripture quotations are from the New Revised Standard
Version of the Bible, Anglicized Edition, copyright © 1989,
1995 by the Division of Christian Education of the National
Council of the Churches of Christ in the USA. Used by
permission. All rights reserved.

Printed and bound in England by
CPI Group (UK) Ltd, Croydon

Contents

Foreword

Every morning I am surprised.

I almost do a double take when I look at the face in the mirror whilst I am shaving and think, 'This is the face of the Archbishop of Canterbury.' Behind this is not a doubt that God has called me. It's not even a regret that he has (well, most days anyway). It's that I can't quite believe God could use a person like me.

But the wonder of the gospel is that people like me and you are called to follow Jesus and are used in his service. What he requires of us is obedience and faith, not multi-competence and self-certainty.

Often when we hear the word 'Pioneer', we think of someone who we don't usually know, or just saw fleetingly on a stage before they went off to inspire another crowd. Someone who is a make-it-happen person. Someone who blazes their trail and doesn't have a shred of doubt or incompetence but brings what others can only dream about into reality. In our minds a pioneer is a super-hero figure who, whilst breathing the same air as mortals, doesn't really let their feet touch the same ground.

This thinking doesn't help us, because very few of us are like this, maybe 1 in 100, 000. And because most of us aren't like this we assume it's just other people who can be involved in the pioneering work of God. And so we don't count ourselves into the fresh things of God.

But we know the church of Jesus Christ desperately needs to be taken forward not simply maintained.

This is why I really rate this book. In it each of us hear a call which involves us in the new things the Holy Spirit is doing. This is a 'Can do' book, a book best put into the hands of people who sense a desire to respond to the call of God to reimagine things, but don't quite know the steps to realise it. It is deeply practical, deeply hopeful and deeply involving.

In reading it we will be confronted once again by the God who miraculously calls his church into being in the lives of ordinary men and women who are simply obedient to do what He calls us to. The local church is the hope for every community. For it is among us that the life of Jesus Christ is made visible. The wine of the Spirit takes on the shape of the wineskins. These wineskins are our life together.

I pray fervently that the fruit of this book would be God's pioneering work of building his church in neighbourhoods and networks, in parishes and amongst people who keep wondering with amazement that God has chosen to use people like them to do things like this.

Justin Welby
Archbishop of Canterbury

Preface

I realized about a year ago that there was no simple book available that I could give to people who wanted to start a new small Christian community that was for and with those who did not normally go to church. So I have set out to write a guidebook that will help people get started, especially if they are not sure how to proceed.

One of my strong convictions is that many people can do this. You don't need to be a church professional, or particularly holy or highly theologically trained. It really is not 'rocket science'. I believe that, with a few basic principles and practices and the right kind of support and backing, many more people could start something new. If we want to see Jesus' Church made much more accessible to people in their workplaces, social lives, networks, neighbourhoods and community activities we need thousands more of these kinds of communities in every place and area.

We have to be realistic about the statistics, which tell us that the majority of people are unlikely to go to their local church as it now exists, however good it is. So we need to develop church where people live their everyday lives and that connects with them, where they are. I have been involved in these kinds of communities for over 20 years. With a small group of friends I was involved in starting the Net Church in Huddersfield which was created specifically to connect with people who did not go to church. I did this for nine years before moving to train people, lay and ordained, across the UK and internationally to develop and lead these kinds of new communities.

I really hope and pray that this book might encourage you to take the step of starting something new. Together we can make a real difference. Please read the book and, above all, give it a go!

The Church of England Pioneer website, www.cofepioneer. org, has links to this book with further information and stories.

Acknowledgements

Thank you to all the people who in many different ways have contributed to this book. Thanks to all my colleagues in Ministry Division and Fresh Expressions and all the stimulus of former colleagues and students from Cambridge, A block and the CPL team. For the pioneers on a Friday morning a special thanks for allowing me to try out some of this material on you. The advice and encouragement of many small community leaders whom I have talked to has spurred me on to write this. Thanks to all the leaders and participants on my local MSM course – much of the thinking for this book started on those Tuesday evenings. Also to Church House Publishing for their encouragement to do this book. Finally, to my wife Heather, who as always has encouraged and enthused me, especially when the writing was not easy.

1

Introduction
Setting the scene
for the book

Jill has a seven-year-old child who attends the local primary school near her house. She looks forward to the brief moments each day when she chats with other parents at the school gate. Some of them have become great friends. In a busy day it's an oasis of normality for Jill. These people know she goes to the local church. Sometimes Jill wonders if these parents would ever come with her to the local church. She loves the church but it seems culturally so different to their lives. Many of them are busy on Sundays with football, swimming or shopping. What can she do?

Philip and Jen host a book club in their house on the first Tuesday of every month. They often get 15 people crammed into their small lounge. The group started with one other couple. It has expanded as word of mouth got round the village. Conversation about the books is so varied and rich. Even when the group disagree wildly about a book, it's great fun and no one takes it personally. They count down the days to the next meeting. If only they felt the same way about church. The people at church are great. But maybe if it could be more like the book club many more people from the village would attend. What can they do?

James runs an under-14s local football team. He has been the manager for the last seven years. He is certainly no José Mourinho but they did finish runners-up in League 3 last season. He has got to know the parents well too. They are essential for transporting the team and providing hot drinks on match days. Sometimes James feels guilty that he does this on Sundays when he (and maybe the players) should be in church. He has talked to his vicar about how conflicted this makes him feel. He would be delighted if some of his players and maybe their families might come to church. What can he do?

Lillian is the vicar of a growing church in a city suburb. She has been at the church for the last five years. In the parish is a large area of social housing. Despite many more people attending the church during Lillian's time, no one from this area attends the church. To get to the church building they need to cross a large road. It seems to act as a psycho-logical barrier. Once or twice people have ventured into the church. They seem very uncomfortable in the building and have never returned again. The Church Council have regularly asked Lillian why no one attends from the estate. Lillian knows some of the estate people well and wonders what she can do about the situation.

Michael works in a factory. He has worked there most of his life. Many of his co-workers have become close friends over the years. He is also a churchwarden of his local church. Often he feels that these are two very separate worlds and they will never meet. Yet he would love to see some of these friends connect with Jesus. They sometimes have spiritual discussions about things like ghosts, life after death or suffering, but he wonders what else he could do for them.

Juliet hosts a support group each month for families who have lost a young child. She herself lost her daughter during childbirth only three years ago. She was desperate and then discovered this support group. It was the group and her faith that got her through a very dark time. Often the group ends up discussing spiritual questions. 'Where is God in all this?' is often a recurring theme. Juliet wishes she knew of a church that she could take some of these people to. If only it could help them to process the deep questions they grapple with. She feels that too quickly her church wants to give the right answers but leaves no space for doubt or questions. But what can she do?

I know these people. They are real people who were asking what they could do to help the people around them connect with God and find some help with their spiritual concerns and questions.

These seven people are very different in terms of their age, background, gender, education, personality and where they live. There are, though, four key things that are common to all of them.

1 They feel inadequate

This may not be where you thought this list would start. Most of these people found themselves asking the questions but, to be honest, hoped they were not the answer. Some had been Christians for a long time, one of them for less than a year. They often felt their own faith was weak or weary. Some of them were not even thought of as leaders in their own churches. Most of them have had no theological training or even been on any kind of church training course. That sense of inadequacy is often a characteristic seen in those God calls in the Bible. Think of David, Moses or Peter. Great heroes of the faith. They felt they were not up to it. They all argued with God, that surely he had someone better he could use. They felt they had very little to offer, and told God this. But this doesn't seem to be a barrier to God. He loves to use such people. He wants to use us as we are, with all our weaknesses and strengths.

2 They follow the Spirit

They might not use these exact words or even understand all that was happening. In different ways, as they met with people outside the Church, they began to sense God's Spirit was somehow at work. He was prompting them to ask questions about the people God had placed in their lives; people who lived near them, work colleagues, or people who shared interests, hobbies or experiences. They began to be open to the thought that the Holy Spirit might be in this, in the thick of the groups they were part of, or in the friends they were making. It began to dawn on them that he had put them with these people for a reason. He wanted to connect more with these people and was enlisting their help to do so. This meant following the Spirit out into their community, into their homes, workplaces, schools or even a football pitch. These people, through the Spirit's work of prompting them, were willing to take up the challenge to find out how.

3 They fall into God's mission

They discovered a key fact about God. He is not locked up in any one building. He is on the move always. He is at work in the lives of many people in all communities, calling them to connect with him. It dawned on them that God loves people outside the Church. None of them would use the word 'missionary' to describe themselves. But they are all God's missionaries, not in some foreign country but in their neighbourhood. Often unintentionally, they have found themselves caught up in God's activity, which is happening all around them. We follow a God who in Jesus broke out from heaven to be with us. We then see throughout the Bible his people breaking out so that others might discover this loving God. So Israel breaks out of Egypt, the first church breaks out of the Temple, and then the church breaks out into the Gentile world. This pattern continues throughout church history, through the monastic movement planting new churches, the Wesleys taking the gospel to the working classes, or slum priests living in the toughest parts of our cities.

God's call to break out continues today. The Church is breaking out in many new places, not asking people to 'come' to church but taking church to them. Variety is the key. It is breaking out in new places and new ways, and maybe God wants you to be part of this. Your part in the break-out process might not take you to foreign lands or the inner city. The breakout for you may mean a short distance, but it could be a radical step. It may be that God is calling you to step across your street, to step into your community centre, to start something in your own lounge, or begin something different in your church buildings. It might be a short distance, but it is a big step!

4 They found some principles to help them

So what can I do? This is a question that many people are asking. They are aware of many people throughout their lives who want to connect with God. But they also know that most of them will never darken the door of a church. Not because of the local church, but because it's 'not them', it's not what they do, or they are not available during the church's opening hours. Now, imagine that across your country thousands of people have asked the same questions but are able to do something about it. Imagine that we could learn from all these experiments and then discern some principles to help us do the same.

The great news is that this is happening right now. It is estimated that there are over 2,000 of these experiments happening now in the Church of England and many more in other countries, denominations and streams. Often these are called 'fresh expressions of church' and they are happening everywhere. Most of the major denominations are using the language of fresh expressions, and define a fresh expression as 'a form of church for our changing culture, established primarily for the benefit of people who are not yet members of any church'.

Essentially these new communities are

- **Mission-centred**
  They aim primarily to focus on and connect with those outside the Church.

- **Adapting to the context**
  The newly emerging community is shaped with and for the people it is connecting with.

- **Forming disciples**
  The aim is not to get people to attend events but to enable people to discover and follow Jesus together.

- **Creating Jesus-centred communities**
  Such communities are not bridges to existing church, but they create church in the midst of people's lives.

The exact terminology you might use doesn't really matter. What is crucial is that the people leading such things started by asking that simple question, 'But what can I do?'

Most people leading these, lay or clergy leaders, have never done anything like this before. But they are discovering they can. There are some simple principles to follow, which experience has shown work in a huge range of situations. This is often about small groups of people, anywhere between four and forty, who come together to connect with each other and God in a myriad of creative ways that do not require lots of resources.

If you have started this book thinking 'Can I do this?', I want to encourage you that with God's help and a few basic principles you *can*! This is not just for the spiritual elite, the really holy, the very experienced or the professionals. I really believe most people can do this. There are lots of Jills, Philips, Jens and Jameses who are doing this today. Maybe God is inviting you to join him in a mission adventure in your locality or community.

The rest of this book will take you through the principles you need to start something new. It will start from the very beginning of discovering what might be possible in your area, right through to establishing a viable new community growing and developing disciples of Jesus. It will give you clear guidelines and practices that can make your dreams come to life. It is packed full of tried and tested tips. It really is not that difficult, so give it a go. The book assumes no prior knowledge of the principles or a deep understanding of theology. My assumption in writing this book is that this is not your full-time occupation. You are thinking of doing this alongside your main work or study. You may well be doing this in response to your experiences at work, college, in your neighbourhood or area. You might even be doing this alongside your main role of running an established church.

The exciting part is that in putting these principles into practice you are working with God who is already ahead of you. This means that in doing this you will be involved in seeing people's lives changed by a loving God. What could be better? What could be more fulfilling?

Maybe you could read this book with a couple of other interested people and use the questions at the end of each chapter. The key points and questions will help you focus on the important issues as you begin this adventure in mission. You could read the book all at once or work on particular chapters as they become applicable in your own context.

Here is an important warning as you begin the book. There is one thing the book does not do. It will not give you a step-by-step 'one size fits all' model you slavishly follow. Your situation is different from other people's situations. So this book will give you simple principles and practices you can easily apply to your own situation. But you will need to do the work of taking those principles and working out with others how they apply in your particular context. I cannot predict the shape these principles will take in your place, but I can confidently assure you the principles will work. Be encouraged that these principles are already working in thousands of ways up and down this country.

Why not read the rest of the book, use your imagination and see where God might be taking you in his amazing mission adventure for your community, network or neighbourhood. It will be exhilarating, scary and stretching all at the same time, as God leads you forward.

2

The art of seeing

I wonder what has brought you to this point.

- It might be that you are responding to a situation in your locality.
- You might be asking the simple question, that there must be a 'better way' to do church here for those outside the Church.
- You might have stumbled into this, thinking you were starting something else and then finding it might lead to an evolving community.
- You have been praying about your local area and now feel you need to do something.
- Or someone else might have asked you to do this, maybe your vicar or minister.

Whatever has brought you here, this is a really energizing place, but it is also very frightening. When we started the Net Church in Huddersfield I asked the small starting team on our first ever meeting, 'What most excites you and what most scares you?' They all said, 'The answer is the same to both questions. It's starting with a blank piece of paper. "We could do anything" is a great place to be, but it's also a very daunting place.'

You may be starting at this point on your own or with a small group. It will be better if there are at least a few of you. The good news is that you are not really starting from a blank piece of paper. God has been, and is, at work before you and ahead of you. So your main task is *not* to find out what you must do but to see and discover what God is up to in your locality and then start working with him. Relax – this isn't your mission or 'your thing' but God's, and he will help and guide you.

The artist Henri Matisse said, 'To look at something as though we have never seen it before requires great courage.' This is what you need to do with your local community or network you are working in. It's not easy, especially if you know it well. You think you know it already, but do you really?

What you might need at this stage are some conversation partners to help you work out what God is up to.

Here are four possible partners for your conversation.

1 **God**

Talk to him through prayer, and scour Scripture to see what he might be saying to you. The passage that really spoke to us was Genesis 12, the call of Abram and Sarai. These early pioneers in the Old Testament followed

God's call to go even though God had not told them where this eventually might take them. They set out in obedience not knowing their final destination, but with God's promise he was with them and would bless them. This very much felt like our situation; we were setting out on something God had called us to do, but it was very unclear to us at the beginning where it might lead. We had a vague sense of what this might all look like, but we were not sure. God was asking us as a group to leave the comfort and safety of what we knew and to venture out with him into the unknown. Except, of course, it is known to God!

2 **Your context**

What do you know and not know about the place where you are or the network you are involved in? What does the physical space tell you about this area? What about the social environment? Who lives here and what are they like? And what about the spiritual issues in this place? Where do you sense that Jesus is good news for this community? Where might Jesus challenge the community? What are the present values of the community? One of the easiest ways to find out is to host an evening, with food, for people you know in the community to tell you what they think about the community. It is important to listen very attentively at this stage. This is particularly important if you know the area well yourself. Don't assume you know all the answers because you know the place well.

3 **Your evolving community**

As you begin to form an initial team, meet regularly to share and review what you are seeing and learning. Talk together about what you are discovering from others and each other. Are there important things that are surprising or disturbing you? How does what you see in your context relate to what you are reading in Scripture? It is important that the community is not dominated by just one person's viewpoint, but that you are learning together. As you talk about these things together you will start to discern together what God is saying to you. This does not happen in one meeting but may take months as you work together. Prayer is vital throughout the whole process but it is particularly required at this stage. Praying together reminds the community that this is ultimately God's work and you are dependent on him. This is not about coming up with a good plan but discovering God's plans for you and your place. Make sure you pray together regularly as a community and encourage people to pray when you are not meeting together. If people are not used to praying out loud it can help to use some liturgy, which helps people to articulate their feelings and longings.

4 **The Church**

Your local church and the wider church may have some wisdom for you. It is important that you consult with the leaders in your local church. They will have wisdom that will benefit you, and you may even learn lessons from how this Church got going. Conversations with the other churches in your area mean that they are aware of what you are doing and can support and encourage you. They may need reassuring that you're not setting up a rival church or that you are not judging what they are doing. They can also pray for you and may be able to support you in practical ways.

Many of the questions you are asking are not new but have been asked before over the last 2,000 years. It might be worth asking where church history could help you think about what you are trying to do. Where might other break-out movements have something to say to you?

With these key conversation partners it is worth considering the ways God might be guiding you and beginning to form your practices and principles. How might God be speaking to you as individuals and as a community through these partners?

1 **Inspiration**
   What is God saying directly to you in and through this process? This might come through Scripture, prayer, meditation or God planting ideas in your minds.

2 **Investigation**
   What facts, figures, views and ideas are you learning from this process so far? What questions are being formed for you out of these investigations?

3 Intuition

This area is not to be discounted. What is your gut feeling? How are you sensing where God is at work in your area? Often in starting out, this is really important. This is why working with a few others can help as you can share and check your intuition together. It is strange how often leaders improvise their way to creating community which in retrospect feels somehow planned out for them.

4 Imagination

You need to trust the thought in your head that says, 'I wonder what would happen if we …'. Imagining what might be is a really important step in finding your way forward.

5 Experimentation

Try something small scale to see if it might help you develop something for the long term. This could be as simple as hosting a meal for some people or gathering together a few people at the local pub. These interactions will give you clues about what might be possible in the future.

This should begin to help you understand the answers to five simple questions:

1 What's going on in your community?
2 What's going on behind what's going on?
3 What's going on with God in what's going on?

4 What might you do in response to this?
5 How might you begin to make this happen?

The twin dangers

My experience of working with hundreds of leaders in your situation is that there are two opposite dangers at this initial point.

1 **Not leaving enough time**
   When we held our first ever national gathering of leaders like you we asked them what would be the one piece of advice they would give to other leaders. They almost all replied, 'We wish we had taken longer to get going – we started too quickly.' There can be a real danger of rushing in and not taking the time to discern what God is doing in your area. There is a real passion to start something, to begin a group, but the danger is that you don't begin in the right place or the right way. And it's hard to reverse from a false start. The danger is that a false start will mean your team loses confidence or, even worse, starts thinking about quitting.

2 **Never actually starting**
   This is the opposite and equal danger. You want to know exactly what to do and how to do it before you are willing to begin. The danger of this attitude is that you will never start. Understand that you do not need to know everything before you start. You just need to know

enough. You may not know exactly what you are creating will look like in three years' time, but you suspect you have a good sense of what will happen over the first three months. That is enough to get going. I meet lots of people with great ideas who have never done anything with them. At some point you have to take the risk to plunge in and have a go.

There is a real place for learning through experimentation. Don't be scared to say, 'Let's try this for three months.' Then review and make changes if necessary, or even try something completely different. Let me assure you that you will learn as much from what doesn't work as from what does. James Dyson created 5,000 prototype Dyson cleaners before he got it right and then he had to launch Dyson Ltd to produce his design when no other manufacturer would take it on. Remember: in this there are no failures, only prototypes that teach you every time if you are ready to see and listen. Don't be too cautious and end up doing nothing.

There is an important balance to be struck between getting going too quickly and never actually beginning. Each situation is different. There are no easy timescales I can give you. But as long as you are aware of the twin dangers, this should help you not to fall into either trap.

Finally, it's important to understand that all we have been talking about is not preparation for mission but is part of God's mission already. You will discover through this process of conversation God speaking to you in many varied ways.

- A team is being formed and you are discovering who is in this with you. You may find through the various conversations that people suddenly emerge who want to be part of what you are doing. Or you might have a sense that you should ask certain people to join you in what you are hoping to achieve.

- You are understanding where God is ahead of you and you are seeing your locality through his eyes. This is not just about your clever plans, but working in partnership with God who is leading and guiding you in his mission.

- Values are being established through the ways you meet together in these initial days which will shape the new community. A new community is being formed in the way you carry out your investigations.

- Gifts, talents and passions are being discovered through this whole process, which can be harnessed for the future good of the community. People will be trying new things and discovering they have abilities that have been untapped until now.

- Key people might be identified through this process in your area or neighbourhood whom God is calling you to work with and through. Be alert for these people who are supportive of what you are doing even though they are not part of the Church. It may be that God is already working in them and that they may be key for the future of your endeavour.

- You are already discovering that some small-scale experiments in your area are being generated as you talk with and listen to people outside the Church.

The art of seeing, this initial phase, can seem very messy at times. The future will not always be crystal clear at this juncture. You will need to live with uncertainty, disorder and confusion. But you need to remember that God is at work in this stage. You do not need to know everything to start. You only need enough to take those first steps and trust God to guide you the next few steps. This is a risky business, but surely that is what faith is about.

The key things to remember

- God has been and is at work before you and ahead of you.

- You need to trust that thought in your head that says, 'I wonder what would happen if we ...'.

- There is a real passion to start something, to begin a group, but the danger is that you don't begin in the right place or the right way. It's hard to reverse from a false start.

- Understand that you do not need to know everything before you start. You just need to know enough.

- You will learn as much from what doesn't work as from what does.

- God wants to incorporate who you are, your passions and what you do, into his plans and mission.

- It's absolutely vital that you start with the right questions before you start with particular models of how to do it.

- It's important to understand that all we have been talking about is not preparation for mission but is part of God's mission already. Nothing is wasted!

Some important questions to consider

- Who are your conversation partners?

- What's going on in your community?

- What's going on behind what's going on?

- What's going on with God in what's going on?

- How is the balance for you between rushing in and being over-cautious?

Case study
Missional Church, Acton Vale, London

James is part of a missional community in Acton Vale which began when seven young people moved on to an estate in Acton Vale with the intention of helping the people who live there to become disciples of Jesus. The tough estate has a vibrant mix of nationalities and its fair share of social and health issues.

James has a real passion for those on the margins of society. He has been on an exciting and messy journey. Initially a conventional life as a graduate manager changed dramatically when he made a huge decision to leave this career behind. He was volunteering as a church outreach youth worker one or two evenings a week in Acton, as a hobby, from 2003. In 2007 he made his hobby into his job, becoming a full-time youth worker. This brave decision led him to a number of new roles as he developed various projects in Acton. This was, first, with local churches, and then he worked with Brent Social Services as a youth worker in a family support team, working to keep children and teenagers out of care and stay within their family networks.

He has created a social enterprise called BLAZE, a youth employment pilot project which helps young people to find employment. With a local church

youth worker, he began in 2013 building relationships with street drinkers and others. They found
that this brought people to the surface who would
never normally have any contact with the church.
This led to a tailor-made Alpha course that had to be
translated into Polish for some of the people attending. This in turn led to a small-group meeting of
these people in a local coffee shop. Building relationships has involved dealing with mental health and
addiction issues.

James would admit that there has been lots of trying things out and learning in the doing. Flexibility
and experimentation have been key. He has invested
his life heavily in Acton. The values that underpin
James' life and work are prayer, being willing to
try things, meeting people's practical needs so they
make a difference to people's lives, and intentional
evangelism with those way outside the normal orbit
of the Church.

3

Developing a team

This is not a solitary activity. It is not something to do on your own. You need people with you. People who share your vision and are committed to bringing something into reality with you, even if you are not sure exactly what it is yet. Getting the right people together will often be a key factor in the success of what you are trying to achieve.

If you don't have a team of people with you, then your ideas will struggle to blossom. If you have the wrong people with you, again your ideas will struggle to blossom. You can see therefore why a team is so important.

There are often patterns or stages that emerge at the beginning of something new. I wonder if you recognize this pattern in your own story.

Stage 1: dissatisfaction

This is a strong sense you have and maybe others share: something is not working well or could work much better. For me this was a stage that probably lasted five or six years. At the beginning, I don't even think I could properly articulate it. There was just a nagging sense that there must be a way to do church better that would resonate with my friends, neighbours, family and work mates who did not go to a church presently. It's not that the two churches I attended over this period in two different towns were bad or failing churches. One church was in the middle of a large council estate and the other was in suburbia. They were full of good people. One was a very vibrant church, with over 100 children in the Sunday school. But I could not get rid of the feeling that in two very different social areas, one church small and the other very large, both had been created for the people in the church. This great community was set up to look after us and to provide what we wanted, not necessarily what we needed. But there was very little sense of the church being there for people who did not regularly attend it, or the church being part of God's mission to this local community. Of course we talked about encouraging others to join us, and even sometimes did mission events. But I realized that the underlying message was that this was for us – do come and join us but you will have to fit in with us. If you can do this then you are very welcome.

But now the majority of people in this country do not go to church and are not even thinking about going. So if we carry on 'as usual' the only result will be continuing demise. And that is what has happened in these two churches!

Stage 2: a new journey of alternatives

This can be a dangerous stage, as the realization that the present way of working is not effective can easily lead to disengagement. I see this reality in many of my contemporaries who have given up on church even if they haven't given up on their faith. But the good news is that in our small positive reactions we can help to create a different and fresh story.

This can be an exciting stage of realizing that there might be a story other than the one we are presently living. The impetus for this can come from many sources if we have our ears and eyes open wide. For me it was a headline in the local paper and hearing about a church that was doing it differently. The headline was that 53 per cent of people in my town had no contact whatsoever with any religious institution. It shocked me greatly that this was now the new majority. It made me wonder how we ever allowed this to happen. Then I heard about a church that was specifically trying to connect with those outside the Church and had committed to make this their priority. It wasn't that I would or could ever copy what they were doing, but they inspired me to try something.

The key part of this stage is the realization that there are alternatives. There are different stories that can be discovered and explored. The story we are living is not the only possible one!

Stage 3: confirmation and approval

This is the stage where a team comes in. This is where you need other people who confirm what you are thinking. But more than simply agree with your thinking, what you really need is people who will understand what you are thinking and then say, 'Let's do something together to make this a reality.' This is where team really starts.

This team you are recruiting or part of is basically a 'start-up team'. You may require different types of team as things develop, but initially a small group of people is required to get this thing off the ground. By 'team' I simply mean a group of people with an agreed purpose to work together to achieve something that they could not do on their own. This team could be as small as 2 and as big as 20 or 30, depending on the size of what you are trying to begin.

Jesus followed this principle of team. He chose and called 12 others to be his start-up team. He realized he could not do this alone but needed others around him to work with him and to continue and develop his Kingdom work.

So the two key questions you need to consider are:

1 What kind of people do you need?
2 What kind of team do you need?

What kind of people do you need?

The big danger here is thinking first in terms of talents and gifts. I have discovered this is not of first importance. The key people may not be the cleverest, the best musicians, the most experienced leaders or even the most creative people.

1 **People who share your vision and can help further refine it**
It's more about what you see than what you can do.

All my experience tells me this is absolutely crucial. You need people who share your vision or your 'new story'. This does not mean they agree with you in every detail of what you are proposing, but in broad terms you are on the same page. For me this comes a long way before what talents these people can bring to the venture. This takes relational time to discover. This is where having coffee together and talking and dreaming is important. Through conversations you begin to discover if you are going in the same direction. Getting it right at this point can save months and even years of anguish down the line. Where I have seen new ventures failing or not working effectively there was often at these initial stages not a real sense of a shared vision.

This can be difficult for the person or people with the original vision because, as they share it, parts of it might change as it morphs into the team's vision. There will probably need to be some modification and redefining. The idea is now offered to the team and some sense of control is therefore given up. But this is vital as the idea or vision moves from an individual to a team. It must be a vision the whole start-up team shares.

2 Servant-hearted

It's more about who you are than what you can offer.

The character of the people is vital in such a new venture. The basic inclination needs to be, 'This is not about what I can get out of this, but what I can give.' Starting something new will put you all under pressure and you need a team that will and can react positively to this. You need people who are simply willing to put others first. You need to ensure people are not involved just because this is the new thing on the block.

3 Risk-takers

It's more about what you are willing to give up than what cannot be changed.

I have discovered that when it comes to church we all have a default position of what 'proper church' looks like. It often comes from a mixture of our experiences, temperament and personality. We all have such a position and there's nothing wrong with that. But the problem comes when we decide that our default position is really the only way! That immediately leads to problems as it closes down any discussion because there are no alternatives. The team must be ready to step outside their own comfort zone in order to discover new possibilities and serve their community.

The values of risk-taking teams

- **Curiosity**
  The desire to discover and find out new things and new ways. It's all about asking the right kinds of questions even when you have no idea of the answers.

- **Creativity**
  It's about asking how you generate an approach that allows lots of space for the kind of creative thinking that encourages people to see things in new and fresh ways.

- **Contextualization**
  What works in one place or area might not work in your place. It's about deeply understanding where you are so you can dream appropriately.

- **Chance**
  It's about the ability to live with the realization that there is a chance this will not work. But even if it doesn't work at first, lessons are learnt and new possibilities are discovered. This is more about prototypes than failures.

- **Courage**
  It's not just about having ideas, but about being bold enough to follow them through and do something.

What kind of team do you need to be?

- **A relational team**

  A recent business study suggested that the best predictor of productivity is the energy and engagement of the team outside its formal meetings. This does not mean you should all be alike in terms of age or temperament or be good friends before you become a team. But you need to learn how to relate with and to each other. This will involve understanding yourself and each other. It takes time and means spending time together, but it's worth making the investment. There are no shortcuts with relationships. The quality of your relationships will be the bedrock of the relationships in the new community.

- **A trusting team**

  Trust is the glue for the relationships of any team. If you don't trust each other you are in big trouble from the start. But trust does not magically appear. It needs to be developed and modelled by key leaders. Trust is about being willing to ask for help. It involves admitting weaknesses and mistakes to the group. It consists of often offering and accepting apologies without any hesitation. Questions need to be welcomed and risks taken in offering feedback and assistance. Trust is risky and can of course be abused, but it is absolutely essential.

- **An open team**

  Members of the team or group must not be precious or protective. People must feel free to disagree and say what they really feel. This means that ideas and the overall vision can be properly debated and discussed and that nothing is off limits. If the team trusts each other they will be willing to do this to create a future that is more than the sum of any one individual's ideas.

- **A committed team**

  Lastly, the team needs to be committed to the vision and to each other. If there are good relationships, trust and openness will naturally happen. Things will not disintegrate when the going gets tough. People will be willing to commit energy and time to this task. This group of people will make things happen in a creative and innovative way.

So what is the role of the key leader or leaders in helping this to happen?

- **Set the relational temperature.**

  You need to spend time getting to know the team if you don't know them well. Not just in meetings but over a coffee or a meal, or by doing some joint activity.

- **Be self-aware.**

  The best leaders know their own weaknesses, preferences and personalities. Weak leaders ignore them. Being self-aware means you are not threatened by others' ideas, strengths or strategies. In fact you will see winning not as getting your own way or idea agreed but as the team together working out the best way forward.

- **Make the best use of each other's abilities.**
  Discover what people are good at and give them responsibility and support to do it. It is exciting to see team members fully discovering and utilizing their abilities and gifts.

- **Give lots of feedback.**
  Make sure people don't feel alone in what they are doing. Tell them how they are doing and give suggestions for development and improvement. Make sure you are encouraging people as much as possible. Formally and informally find out how people are doing with their roles in the group. If they need further help or training, help them to find where this might be available.

- **Always celebrate success.**
  However small, make sure you celebrate what is happening. It's very easy to pass quickly on to the next thing without commending the team for what is happening. Encourage the habit of celebration pervading all that is going on. One of the best things we ever did was to have a big party of celebration each year. It was the moment to look back and hear lots of stories from people about what was happening and what God was up to. Our celebrations were like a big birthday party for the church.

- **Find a sustainable rhythm.**
  It takes a lot of energy to get something new off the ground. You need to ensure that the leadership life you are living is sustainable. There will be busy times and emergencies but you need to consider how there are also quiet and down times. You will need to discover a

monthly and yearly rhythm as a team which means that leadership is life-giving rather than life-sapping. You can find out more about this in Chapter 9.

Above all, remember you can't do this on your own. You need to find the right people to join you in this mission adventure. When you get the right people together, amazing things begin to happen.

The key things to remember

- If you don't have a team of people with you, then your ideas will struggle to blossom.

- The key part of this stage is the realization that there are alternatives. There are different stories that can be discovered and explored.

- What you really need are people who will understand what you are thinking but then say, 'Let's do something together to make this a reality.'

- Jesus followed this principle of team. He chose and called 12 others to be his start-up team.

- It's more about what you see than what you can do.

- The basic inclination needs to be, 'This is not about what I can get out of this but what I can give.'

- The team must be ready to step outside their own comfort zone in order to discover new possibilities and serve their community.

- The quality of your relationships will be the bedrock of the relationships in the new community.

- When it comes to church, we all have a default position of what 'proper church' should look like.

- Trust is the glue for the relationships of any team. If you don't trust each other you are in big trouble from the start.

Some important questions to consider

- Who is your team?

- How is the size of your team impacting what you are doing? What are the advantages and disadvantages of your current team size?

- Do you share the same vision?

- Are you a risk-taking team? Do you share the five characteristics highlighted in this chapter?

- How well do you relate together, both formally and informally?

- Do you trust each other, and how do you show this?

- How are your relational strengths seen in the developing community?

Case study
Rural parishes in Norfolk

The bringing together of parishes into a team and the loss of stipendiary clergy is usually seen as a step in managing decline. But this is very far from the truth for a group of rural churches in Ely Diocese.

Ken is a self-supporting minister and the rest of his four-person ministry team, which works across five parishes, consists of licensed lay ministers and authorized lay ministers, with two of them still in training. The youngest member of the team is 64! Working together they have brought transformation through their vision of reaching out to the local community rather than only serving those who come to the church.

Across the five parishes they are running three Messy Churches, including an adults-only Messy Church, plus a men's breakfast club, a lunch club and a youth club. The adults-only Messy Church came from noticing how the adults enjoyed the craft activity at the normal Messy Church. So Ken and one other leader from the team decided to see if they could start an adults-only one. They asked the existing congregation not to come, and quickly had 28 people from the community booked on the first one. They have made it clear that this is a Christian event and the theme is always linked to the Christian faith, with a specific God-time. The creative themes have included bread-making, Advent activities and creating patio pots.

They have tapped into local expertise to help with running the events, and volunteers from the village help. Those attending help to come up with the creative ideas. This new and exciting Messy Church now meets every six weeks.

The ministry team is aided by about 25 volunteers. The team has been greatly helped by the support of the diocese and two of the team have attended the local Mission-Shaped Ministry Training Course.

Through all these various events, Ken estimates that in these rural communities the church is connecting regularly with 300–400 people who do not come to the regular services. It clearly shows that with a vision to look outwards and a dedicated team you can make a huge difference.

4

The art of the start

This chapter is closely linked to Chapter 5, 'Making connections', and the two chapters are best read together as a pair.

There is a real danger that you can spend all your time thinking about what you could do and not actually doing anything. Doing, not thinking about doing, is in the end the essence of pioneering something new. I have met some people who have great ideas about what they could do in their community but never actually get round to doing it.

The key leadership habit at this stage is a willingness to give it a go. If you are thinking things like, 'I would rather try and fail than not try at all', or, 'What have we got to lose if we give this a go?', then you are probably a pioneering leader even if you might not use this title about yourself. The other key skill required at this stage is working out the best idea from a list of ideas. With a group of people you might have come up with ten possible things you could do in your area, but the most important ability is to work out where to begin. You need to start with the right idea. When we began in Huddersfield we had so many ideas: wanting to work with single mums, the homeless, town-centre workers, sports people, and so on. I soon realized that as a small team we couldn't do all this from day one. What was key was to choose the right place to start.

You may have reached the point where you have sensed that God is up to something and you are discovering more about that. The key questions you are asking are: Should we do something in response to this? What exactly should that be? This leads inevitably to questions about how you can make this happen and what the result will be.

It is important to understand that this is not a simple task, but complex. By that I mean there might not be one simple solution to these questions for your particular context. You can't simply do what someone else has done, because your situation is different. You will probably discover your way forward by trial and error. This will call for experimenting, reflecting upon your activities to make sense of what is happening and then refining what you are doing. It means that when you start you will probably not be able to fully describe where this adventure will take you. You will find your way, but not by waiting until you have all the answers. You will discover the answers in the journey, in the doing, in the starting. That's why prayer is so important at this stage as you seek to work with God. Coupled with prayer you need hope. The hope that says change is really possible and we are going to try this with all our energy.

You can certainly learn from the experience and wisdom of others through visiting other new communities, reading books or looking on websites. But you have to adapt this learning to your own context.

This is not complicated. I have discovered that there are three simple principles or habits you need as you start. But as well as having all three they have to operate in the right order for your plans to be effective. It really is as simple as love–relate–create.

Love–relate–create

- **Love**

  This is all about your motivation. It provides the answer to the question of why you are doing this. Ultimately this is not about declining church numbers, financial problems or even an irrelevant church, but it is about love. The foundation for this is that God loves you without any preconditions. He does not love you more because you are thinking of creating a new community. He will not love you less if what you try does not work out exactly as you had hoped. You need to understand this at the core of your being and continually return to this primary motivation. This is why prayer, Scripture, corporate worship and spiritual disciplines are vital as you begin this adventure. They provide opportunities to be reminded that you are loved greatly.

- **Relate**

  'God so loved the world that he gave his only Son' (John 3.16) is part of probably the most famous verse in the Bible. It illustrates that love is not an internal emotion but an attitude that sends you out to relate to others. Love does not turn us in on ourselves but always sends us out into relationships.

  We begin to comprehend as we are loved by God that so are the many people God has put around us. We start to see and understand our family, friends, neighbours, work mates and others in light of God's love for them. This also gives an integrity to our activities. We are doing this because we love as God loves us. People are not targets to get into church but creatures beloved by the Creator. It means that we will go on loving them and relating to them whatever their reactions to our activities. Ultimately what you are doing is based on relationships, God's relationship to you and your relationship to others.

- **Create**

  This is the third stage of asking what you, with others, could do to help people you know to reconnect with God. What would you need to happen to help them have the best opportunity of meeting the God who loves them and you? There are endless possibilities, but what might work for the people you know?

The danger is that we usually get these three principles in the reverse order. We can easily end up with create–relate–love.

So we think about creating something new; it might be our idea or the latest activity we heard about from a conference. We therefore announce we are going to create an event. Then we ask the follow-up question: who can we get to come to this? This then means trying to get to relate to people in our community so we can invite them to this new thing. And then if they do start coming to whatever we are doing we now have to love them!

This might be a bit of an overstatement of what happens when the process is reversed. But if I am honest in the past I have definitely worked on the create–relate–love model. It's not a comfortable model, often using guilt as the main motivation. It can be easy for leaders to imply that, if this doesn't work, this church will not last much longer.

I love what four Christians are doing in a new-build town near Cambridge. They have started something they call the Deckchair Listening Project. They are trying to build relationships in a new town where everyone is new to the community. They regularly set themselves up with deckchairs they have designed in a public area. They sit around and make clear they are available to talk and listen to people's stories and share their own. Out of the amazing conversations this is producing they are wondering what the next step might be in developing a community.

As I read stories about new Christian communities developing I realize they can start from a massive variety of relationships. Some begin through relationships among young mums, some through parents in the schoolyard, through sporting activities, crafts, around meals, dog walkers or people who love the countryside. The good news is that this is not about inventing new things but working out how God might want to use our existing relationships and activities. I recently talked to someone who is creating a new Christian community through his enjoyment of playing board games. He has met many other people locally who share his passion. He has specifically found three people outside the church who want to help him to create this new community, and it's working!

Some key things to remember when starting

- You don't need to know everything before you start, and in starting you will begin to sense the way forward. You are working towards a new future even before that future actually begins to take shape.

- The key is experimentation. Try a few things and see what works, and refine and improve from there. The shape of what you are trying to do will emerge from your reflections on your experiments. There is no failure here, only prototypes. Don't give up too early but be prepared to try and try again. I read recently the story of five people trying to develop community in Whitby. Much of their story is about trying different things that seemed to eventually peter out. They began with some events, which had limited impact. So they then tried using a local cafe as their base, and again it started well but dwindled somewhat. But in trying different things and refining what they were doing they have created an effective community. These five friends have created a community of 40–60 people, which has generated further activities including a youth project.

- There is no simple formula to follow or all-encompassing plans that show you what to do every step of the way. You will feel as if you are making it up as you go along. Do not limit where your prayers and imagination might take you.

- This new emerging community will develop around the relationships and activities the starting team begin.

- Give this new community time to form and gel. Do not be changing things so quickly that nobody knows what's happening. This whole process takes time, certainly months and maybe over a year or two.

- Be thinking about what the emerging identity of the new community is starting to look like. Is there a distinct sense of belonging which is starting to emerge? One good way to discern this is how the people coming to your community activities refer to the group.

- Try as quickly as possible to find ways that the whole community can exchange gifts so that you don't become a group that only does things for others. It is important that you develop a group where you all serve each other. This is about doing activities *with* people rather than *for* them. A great way to feel belonging is to be able to do something for others.

- Are there key stakeholders and partners that you could be working with? Depending on your community, this could be the local council, schools, social services or key individuals who have an important social role where you live.

Finally, it's important to consider how you will describe yourselves. People often ask me when you should mention the Christian or church word. My own advice is as soon as possible. I think there is nothing worse than for people to discover later on that you are linked to a local church, or are a group of Christians. It makes it much harder to introduce spiritual elements if this has not been clear at the start. It also makes people think you must have something to hide if you didn't talk about this early on. This doesn't mean you have to talk about the Christian faith every time you meet in the early days. But it is important to say what your motivation is in doing this. You could say you are doing whatever you are doing as part of the local church or because as a group of people you wanted to respond to God's love for your neighbourhood.

How do we know if this is working?

This is a great question to ask and important to consider, especially when you might be experimenting with lots of different ideas. This way of working around love–relate–create takes a much longer time period than the reverse process. An emerging community may take six months to three years to emerge. So how in this timescale do you know if you are doing the right things? How do you measure whether things are going well? If you are doing this in association with a local church or denomination, how might they want to measure this?

For leaders, expectations are a key element. They need to be realistic. It will mean balancing a variety of expectations – your own, your team's, maybe your communities' and lastly perhaps those of a sponsoring church. The danger is that each of these groups might have different expectations about what should or might happen.

It's important to keep asking questions about what you are doing so that you can reflect and refine what you are doing. But it's worth thinking about who these reflections are for. Is it for your own benefit, or is it for your church, a local agency or denomination? Second, what is the purpose of the questions? Is it for your own learning, or because you need to answer to some other group or body? Finally, you need to think about what is being measured.

Perhaps the most basic question is about numbers. This is valid, but it's not the only question to be asked. Certainly if you have been doing something for three years and nobody has ever joined your new community there might be need for serious reflection. But here are some other possible questions you might like to ask.

- Where do you sense God at work in your community?
- Where do you see signs of God's Kingdom?
- Where are you building relationships in your locality?
- In what ways are you serving your community?
- How do you see community beginning to form?
- What are your hopes and dreams at this point?
- Do you feel your expectations at this stage are being met?
- How would you assess your progress with this new community?
- What is distinctive about your community?

Recent research on new types of Christian communities carried out by the Church Army suggests that small is beautiful. On average the starting group is between 3 and 12, and the average size of a new community is 45. But the startling finding was that over 70 per cent of people attending such communities were people who did not usually go to church. This percentage is the largest of any missionary movement I have ever seen. This isn't about a few large communities but hundreds of small communities that are connecting effectively with people outside the Church. How exciting to be part of this growing movement! (You can find the details of this Church Army research at www.churcharmy.org.uk/

Groups/244966/Church_Army/Church_Army/Our_work/
Research/Database_for_fresh/Database_for_fresh.aspx.)

Preparing for the next stage

It is worth thinking about three important questions to reflect upon as your community begins to develop.

- What assumptions have you built into your community and activities? Which of those are now deemed to be valid and which might need to be adapted or changed? This might be about who you connect with, or what activities work, or where and when you do community.

- Are there important future milestones for your community that might be worth considering? This could relate to how you structure your team, frequency of community/worship activities, or local groups you might connect with.

- Are there specific tasks you need to accomplish as the new community becomes more established? This could be governance issues, financial requirements, safeguarding issues or finding suitable places for community gatherings. There is helpful advice about many issues regarding how to finance a fresh expression at www.parishresources. org.uk.

The key things to remember

- Doing, not thinking about doing, is in the end the essence of pioneering something new.

- You will discover the answers in the journey, in the doing, in the starting.

- It really is as simple as love–relate–create.

- The danger is that we usually get these three principles in the reverse order: create–relate–love.

- The good news is that God wants to incorporate who you are, your passions and what you do, into his plans and mission.

- The key is experimentation. Try a few things and see what works, and refine and improve from there.

- Be thinking about what the emerging identity of the new community is starting to look like.

- For leaders, expectations are a key element. They need to be realistic. It will mean balancing a variety of expectations.

Some important questions to consider

- How do you know when it is the right time to start?

- Can you see the principles of love–relate–create operating in your new community?

- Where are you experimenting? What are you learning from these experiments?

- What might be the appropriate questions you should be asking now about what you are doing?

- What are your expectations for the next 12 months?

- What assumptions you made are being challenged by your experiences?

5

Making connections

Research around developing new Christian communities indicates that one of the biggest lessons we are learning is that worship services or events are not the best place to start if we really want to connect with those outside the Church. We can easily jump straight into trying to make our worship services more relevant. Maybe we start by organizing an event because we have heard it works when other people did it near us. The danger is we imagine if only we had more modern music, or better preaching or more family-friendly services then people would flock back to church. But the reality is that experience and research is teaching us very clearly that starting this way may attract disillusioned Christians but will leave those outside the Church untouched. People in your community are not sitting at home thinking, 'If only my local church's music was better, more modern, traditional or quieter I might go.' They really are not!

The place to start making connections is not an event but in relationships. Where and how can we genuinely love and serve people in our locality? It is these authentic connections that are key to developing new communities. The first-order question is therefore not 'What activity or event should we do?' but, 'Who should we be connecting with?'

I read some books on developing new communities that make it sound as though only professional experts, clergy or particular types of Christians can do this. But my experience is that it's not that difficult, and many so-called 'ordinary' people are doing it. To start, you have simply to answer these three key questions and then get going. And they are not very difficult questions. They are really helpful in thinking about the connections we already have, and how loving and relating might lead to creating something new. (I discovered these questions and ideas through the work of Dr Saras Sarasvathy on entrepreneurship. You can discover more at www.effectuation.org.)

These are the three questions and they are not difficult to answer!

1 Who are we?
2 What do we know?
3 Who do we know?

Who are we?

The really good news is that God wants to incorporate who we are, our passions and what we do, into his plans and mission. Our fear is that God will end up getting us to do something we hate.

So who are you? How would you answer this as individuals and as a group? The answer to this might relate to your age, social life, stage of life, hobbies and pursuits, work or geography. For me, I am now a parent whose children have left home. I have started living on a new estate. I love everything to do with sport. I am a commuter. The list could go on.

What do we know?

What groups, places, societies has God been bringing into your view? What issues, needs, problems, questions has God been speaking to you about? What and who is it God has been putting into your minds and hearts? Where and to whom might you feel God's compassion? These kinds of questions might relate to your geography, the area where you live. But they might also relate to where you work or socialize, or your place of study, and they might not necessarily be close to where you live. They might even relate to the developing online world.

I know one group of Christians who were thinking about what they know. They recognized that the people in their area would not go to church on a Sunday morning because they were all at the local park watching their children playing rugby. Some of these Christians were rugby fans and rugby was a big deal in their community. Instead of complaining about people playing sport on a Sunday in competition with church, they went along to the rugby. It didn't take them long to work out there was one key thing missing at the park. There were often five or six junior rugby matches going on but there were no refreshments. Nowhere for waiting parents to buy a hot drink or sweets for their children. So this group, with the agreement of the rugby club, provided the refreshments every Sunday. Not surprisingly, they developed really good relationships over time with parents and children attending the rugby. This led over the next year to them beginning an all-age service from the growing relationships they had built. This service began monthly after the rugby in a local social club.

The question to ask is, how might who you are and what you know relate together?

Who do we know?

What connections do you have with the people and groups you have been talking about? Who might be the key people to start with? Where has God put you in closest proximity to them?

I know of two new communities that began through relationships formed by dog walking. In the Derby area this was a really important way into the community for a new couple and has eventually led to a community centred on Jesus.

A community in Halifax began providing food and support to people on the margins of society. This help was given with no intention of forming any kind of Christian community. But as they loved and served people, they discovered many of those coming had deep spiritual questions. Out of responding to this, a new Christian community of 50–60 people has developed, but it has taken time.

A speech therapist in Belfast who works with special needs teenagers realized that they would struggle to fit into a traditional church community. So, with some others she started a monthly meeting with the teenagers. The gathering involves everything from sharing news to singing and dancing to enable those present to create a community centred on Jesus.

A couple in Sussex realized many people they knew were at a car boot sale on Sunday and so have set out to create a new Christian community at a car boot sale. This has taken time and, as they commented, required being regular attenders and building up trust. They now have a pitch where people can sit, chat and talk, which is leading to many spiritual conversations.

A couple of people in Cheshire have started something around knitting which is particularly aimed at those over 60. There is conversation, food and prayers. What is knitted is often sent off to those in need around the world.

A friend who has moved to Canada emailed recently to tell me that she and a small team have started Third Space, which is trying to connect with their local business community. They are developing a ministry based on a coffee shop and a wellness centre. The centre offers counselling and life coaching. My friend has used her counselling skills and connected them to a particular part of the community to create something very exciting.

I have heard recently about people starting communities based on allotments, creating a group and providing food for local charities. There are also a whole host of forest churches popping up as new communities are formed with people who find it easier to worship outside. These groups often combine personal transformation and the renewal of creation.

There are so many ways of connecting with people. Let your imagination run wild and think how you might be able to develop the connections you already have in your community to create new Christian communities.

It is absolutely vital that you begin with these three questions before you start with any particular models of how to do it. So don't begin by saying we are going to do a cafe church. Start with answering these questions and then you can ask if there is a model that you could use, like cafe church, which is appropriate to your answers. But you may not have to invent the right response as you see what God is doing in your community.

I often explain that this process is like the way you might cook a meal tonight at home. I am the main cook in my family. There are two possibilities for our meal tonight. One is I could choose a favourite recipe from a cookery book. I would need to ensure I have the correct ingredients and then follow the step-by-step guide to make the dish. Yet, if I am honest, this is not how I usually cook our family meal. What normally happens is I open the fridge door and look at what is in there. Not just at the front, but hidden away in the corners. I might look in the bowls to see what left-overs are also lurking there. Then I try and work out how I might combine these various ingredients to create a tasty and nourishing meal.

What we are talking about in this chapter is not like cooking a meal from a recipe book. You can't just turn to the right page and follow the instructions. The reason this doesn't work is that you have to take account of your own context and locality. There is no quick fix; you have to discover what God is doing in your locality and then discover what is appropriate for your area. It's much more like the cooking method that most of us use. It's the 'fridge' method. How can you combine what God has given you to create something new that connects you to people and to God?

So what do you see when you open your fridge door? What has God given you in terms of people, place and passions? How might he then be calling you to combine these ingredients to make something through which people can find good news in people, community and Jesus? The danger is that we focus on what we haven't got, rather than wonder how we can effectively use our God-given resources. It needs imagination and courage to do something with what you see, but it really is possible to combine your God-given ingredients for his mission in your area.

When we started something new in Huddersfield we started with a small group of us saying that we were young adults in the Church but that there were very few of us in churches across the town. What we knew was that we didn't really feel able to invite our friends to our church. It just didn't really relate to them and it made lots of assumptions that they could not relate to. We knew some of these people well and so asked what kind of community would be attractive to them and would enable them to explore more about God, even if they were not sure if he existed. We started to ask ourselves how we could do this in a way that was relevant to the lives of our friends. We began by trying lots of different ways of connecting with our friends, neighbours, work mates and family. We hosted discussion evenings, organized lots of social activities and projects and had lots of fun sharing meals. Gradually a community began to form around us and is still going 17 years later.

I know some mums in Cambridge who answered these questions. Who were they? They were mums praying for their local school. But then God told them they needed to do something. So what did they know? They knew from their conversations in the playground that many mums in the area were struggling with various form of addiction, loneliness and isolation. Who did they know? They knew some of these mums from the playground. So they started on a Friday morning, offering mums a space to meet in the school after they had dropped their kids off. Gradually they began to build deeper relationships with the mums. Eating breakfast has always been a key part of this group. They started to pray for them and with them and discovered together that prayer works. They watched DVDs about the Christian faith, which gave opportunities for people to discover more about that faith. The mums who were the first to attend then started to invite their friends to come along to this amazing new community. Four years later, two new Christian communities have started from these initial conversations in the playground, and many people's lives and families have been transformed.

I heard recently of some people on a large estate in Southport who had realized that many people around them were both lonely and hungry. They wanted to respond to this situation and they knew some of these people. So they started something called Franky's Pizza as a place where local people could discover food, fun and conversation. They have seen community beginning to form and develop in a tough area.

It is imperative you realize that the success of what you are doing will depend on the quality of relationships much more than on the excellence of any events you host. You need to put your efforts into developing the relationships you have and forming new ones. This chapter provides you with the key questions to ask in developing these relationships and the new community they might lead to.

The key things to remember

- Worship services or events are not the best place to start if we really want to connect with those outside the Church.

- The first-order question is therefore not 'What should we do?' but 'Who should we be connecting with?'

- The really good news is that God wants to incorporate who you are, your passions and what you do into his plans and mission.

- It is absolutely vital that you begin with these three questions before you start with any particular models of how to do it.

- There is no quick fix; you have to discover what God is doing in your locality and then discover what is appropriate for your area.

Some important questions to consider

- How would you describe who you are?

- Who is it God is putting into your hearts and minds?

- Who are the key connections in your community?

- What do you see when you open your fridge door?

Case study
Connections, Saxmundham, Suffolk

You never know what a simple invitation might lead to. Tom, who works for BT, was invited by his in-laws, with his wife, to help at an event the parish church in Saxmundham were putting on. The termly event was created to connect with a new housing estate at the opposite end of the town from the parish church building. It was held in the primary school on the estate.

But Tom realized that the people attending this event were very unlikely to come to the parish church. So he made two big decisions. The first was to move the family to Saxmundham to get involved with the church, and the second, with the support of the church, to start something new for the people who were coming to the termly event. With the help of the curate he began Coffee and Doughnuts. It moved what was happening from an event to a fledgling new community. It operated with cafe-style worship, including a creative mix of film clips, prayer, discussion and Scripture, but with no sung worship. A core group developed from this as new people began to grow as disciples of Jesus.

This led in 2015 to developing Connections, a new community which is part of the parish but which very much has its own identity. The usual attendance is between 45 and 75 including children. Over half the people attending come from the new housing estate. Tom has helped to develop a leadership team and there is a strong group of volunteers who help with the practical elements of running this new church.

This has been an exciting journey for Tom, but often it has not been quick or always easy. Tom has had to discover what is possible when you are doing something like this alongside a full-time job. It has taken ten years to get to this point and things are still developing and evolving as this new church understands more of its mission to the town.

6

Building community around Jesus

> It is surely a fact of inexhaustible significance that what our Lord left behind him was not a book, nor a creed, nor a system of thought, nor a rule of life but a visible community. He committed the entire work of salvation to that community. (Lesslie Newbigin, *The Household of God*, SCM Press, 1954)

This may all seem novel, but what you are doing is simply a continuation of what Jesus started with his 12 friends 2,000 years ago. Last words are usually crucial. Jesus' last words as recorded in Matthew's Gospel, often called the Great Commission, underline this. The 'go therefore and make disciples of all nations' is not primarily about going to a new place (Matthew 28.19). A better translation would be, 'in your going, make disciples of all nations'. In other words, as you live your lives, help people to become my followers in community as I have done with you. The 'all peoples' or 'all nations' has the emphasis of every people group. That is why we need lots of new communities that connect with the huge variety of peoples in today's world. They might be centred on ethnicity, economics, social grouping, interest groups or the workplace. No one should be excluded from having the opportunity to be connected to Jesus.

It is important to understand that this process we are considering is not simply about creating new community groups but about building community that is centred on Jesus. This may make you feel nervous, but stay with me through this chapter as we explore what that might look like. Community begins in the gospel where Jesus is with others in their everyday lives: at the boats of fishermen or the offices of tax collectors. This does not mean that everyone in the community is a signed-up, committed follower of Jesus. It does mean that this community, and therefore those connected to it, are on a spiritual journey in relation to Jesus. This might be towards him or away from him. The community has the band width to cope with this but has a clear aim to help people move closer to Jesus.

In Jesus' new community you see the opening up to possibilities of change and newness. Opening yourself up to Jesus and his community means beginning to see in a new way. Through Jesus the world can suddenly seem much bigger, with a greater potential to see oneself, the world and God differently. The danger in our world is that the possibilities for people's lives are often closed down. The good news is that through Jesus the world can suddenly seem and be much bigger. It is wonderful to consider how your new community can become a local enterprise of vision, transformation and hope. The landscape for the individual and community can look very different.

What we are understanding is that this is a varied journey and that it takes time. People are no longer willing to sign up to a community that says there is only one way to do this journey. It is important that the journey has its own value and integrity.

You see such a community developing in the Gospels. The 12 disciples are on a journey, usually towards Jesus but sometimes they struggle with Jesus. We see situations like Peter's denial of Jesus, or James and John arguing who is to be the most important in the new community. But around this start team we see glimpses of a growing community made up of every type of person. It might be key officials such as Nicodemus, or Mary Magdalene, or the Samaritan woman. Each of their encounters with Jesus is very different.

What you begin to see in Jesus' methods is that telling and living out the good news creates community, but community is crucial in being the crucible where the good news can be experienced, tested and practised. As this happens, this good news community becomes attractive to others who want to discover more about the one at the centre of it.

The rest of the New Testament takes up the values of this new community of disciples when it applies the word *koinonia* to what was happening throughout the Roman Empire as these new Christian communities began to develop. It was a fairly common word, often used to describe corporations, guilds, law firms and even marriages. It is translated in various ways in our English Bibles but has the sense of an active communion, joint participation, sharing or making a contribution. The idea of community in the New Testament is not about meeting together but doing together.

So how do you move from developing a starting group to creating a community centred on Jesus?

This new community will by necessity develop around the relationships, values and activities that the start-up team have created and established. Community will spill out from what has been grown by the start-up team. If it is attractive it will encourage others into it.

So what are some of the hallmarks of such a developing community?

- **It has a number of ways into the community.**
  It is important that there are as many different ways as possible of connecting with the community. It could be through friendship groups, shared activities, worship or social undertakings. The more doors into the community, the more likely you are to create a healthy community.

- **It offers a sense of belonging or identity.**
  What makes people feel they belong to the community? What are the ways people identify themselves with the community? It might be through relationships to the leader or the opportunity to participate in the life of the community. Language can often give a clue. I have found that when people begin to feel they belong they use

words such as 'our' or 'we' about the community rather than 'it' or 'them'. It is important that people feel they matter to each other.

- **It involves influence and participation.**

  It is important that those joining the community feel they can influence it but also that it is influencing them positively. As the group develops, the views and gifts of those joining need to be incorporated into the life of the community. It will help if people have opportunities both to give and receive. How can you incorporate people's gifts, abilities and talents into the community so that from the beginning they feel they can contribute?

- **There is shared emotional connection.**

  This is really important and is part of the intangible sense of belonging. It comes from stories that create connection and that invite others to join the story of the community. As a new community, once a year we would go away for a weekend. The evenings were often filled with fun through the telling of stories about things that had happened to us as a community. Someone might say, 'Do you remember when …?' and then everyone would pitch in with their memories. This kind of connection was deeply attractive to people coming into the community who wanted to be part of this growing emotional connection. The other place where this was seen was in our annual celebrations of the community where storytelling was at the heart of what we did. Anyone could contribute as we looked back over the last year and celebrated all that had happened and that God was doing in the midst of our stories.

- **It gives experience of community centred on Jesus.**
  This is where and how people will begin to move towards the one who is at the centre of the community. It reminds us that ultimately this is his community. This happens informally through living with those who are following Jesus. It comes through the experience of seeing at close quarters how these people live their lives. Hopefully they exude Jesus' values and life through the way they deal with every aspect of their lives. But there is also space for more intentional times to move towards Jesus. This could be centred on particular festivals, celebrations and holidays such as Christmas, Easter, Mothering Sunday or Pentecost. But the community could create its own celebrations that relate to its context. This might include events like the start of the school year, local celebrations, or national events. The use of Holy Communion and baptism is also important in developing the community and centring it on Jesus. We found that communion was particularly powerful because of the participatory nature of the meal. It gave people the chance to be involved in the story of salvation through taking the bread and wine.

- **It gives opportunities to learn the faith, to see in a new way.**
  Jesus' last words included teaching as part of developing new communities. There can be a nervousness about teaching the faith. Yet in a society where people's know-

ledge of the Christian faith is very small this must be important. The most effective way of doing this, though, is probably not through lectures or talks. The most successful way I have found is through small groups getting together, maybe weekly, for four to six weeks to look at some of the stories of Jesus, to interact directly with him and his words. The point of these groups is not for the leaders to teach the group but to learn together from Jesus through the use of good questions. In Huddersfield we found this simple process the best way to help people to move quickly towards Jesus. But it needs to be done in a way that makes people feel after the group has finished that they are still part of the community even if they are not convinced about Jesus. We often found people would join this small group two or three times as part of their spiritual journey.

- **It encourages people to return.**
This journey to Jesus can be complex and confusing for people and so it is vital that the community is open to people and does not necessarily close down conversations and relationships. We discovered in Huddersfield that often people would vanish from the community for some months and we felt they had gone. But then they would return, and we realized that circumstances of their lives led them to disappear for a period of time. It is important to develop a community that leaves its doors open and welcomes people back in. We need communities that are like the prodigal father in Luke 15, who encourages the son's return with open arms and a party.

- **It is patient and mindful of pace.**

  Research suggests that it can easily take people four years to move from vague interest to real commitment to Jesus. How do we build a community that can work with that and does not create an environment that says you have three months to make your mind up about Jesus? We need to allow time for this process of spiritual exploration to develop. We must also give places and times where people can respond to Jesus, not in a forced way but in ways that can appropriately encourage them to say a yes to Jesus however small it may seem. It is also important to recognize that there is not just one prescribed journey to Jesus and to encourage a variety of routes that help people to understand and experience him.

Two important issues relating to developing community need to be considered.

- **Niche communities**

  One of the major criticisms of the development of new Christian communities is that they start with a particular age, interest or social group. Therefore they do not truly represent the diversity that should be present in Christian community, which should be a place where all peoples come together. The simple answer is that such communities might start with people who are similar to each other but they can never remain like that if they are to reflect Jesus' values. My experience is that as communities develop they start to ask how they can serve and connect with people who are not like them. They start to ask questions about other types of people and how they might help them journey towards Jesus. As these new people join the community, it will inevitably change the nature of the community. I remember going to meet those involved in a surfing Christian community near Sydney. For me, one of the signs that Jesus was opening their eyes to the bigger picture was the simple realization that people who were not surfers existed. They were beginning to think about developing support for young people across the community who had literacy problems. This was good news in action.

- **The danger of idolized community**
  The danger is that we end up worshipping the ideal of community rather than Jesus who is at the centre of the community. Implicitly, the message can be received that we are creating a new and perfect community. This is a dangerous message because of course perfect community does not exist. As soon as we are part of it, we will at times break it; that's the nature of humanity. Yet we also want to say positively that life centred on Jesus should look and feel different.

So how do we reconcile these two things? Somehow we need to help people to move towards the reality of good community while being realistic about the limits of human beings in community. The dissonance between the two will hopefully lead the community, not to give up on its values through disappointment, frustration and failure, but to move forward positively to become a growing and developing group of people who are serving God, each other and the wider community. This is why some of the key values of Jesus, like forgiveness, humility and faith, are so crucial in developing realistic community.

The key things to remember

- What you are doing is simply a continuation of what Jesus started with his 12 friends 2,000 years ago.

- Community begins in the gospel where Jesus is with others in their everyday lives.

- In Jesus' new community you see the opening up of possibilities of change and newness. Opening yourself up to Jesus and his community means beginning to see in a new way.

- This new community will by necessity develop around the relationships, values and activities that the start-up team have created and established.

- It is important that those joining the community feel they can influence it, but also that it is influencing them positively.

- This journey to Jesus can be complex and confusing for people and so it is vital that the community is open to people and does not close down conversations and relationships.

- We need to allow time for this process of spiritual exploration to develop, but we must also give places and times where people can respond to Jesus.

- Somehow we need to help people to move towards the reality of good community while being realistic about the limits of human community.

Some important questions to consider

- How do you understand the idea of community centred on Jesus?

- In what ways is your community becoming a local enterprise of vision?

- What makes people feel they belong to the community?

- Where might people learn about the Christian faith in your community?

- How are you leaving your doors open for people to return?

- How are you recognizing both the promise of good community and the reality of human community?

Case study
Fur Clemt cafe, Wigan

Ann, who attends the parish church and works for a property company in Wigan, has been on a huge journey over the last two years.

It started in August 2014 with a small-scale response to 'holiday hunger' for children in Wigan over the long summer holidays. Ann had been inspired by the work of the Real Junk Food Project in Leeds and borrowed many of their ideas to find sources of food to feed children and young people. The Real Junk Food Project is an organic network of pay-as-you-feel cafes. They divert food destined for waste and use it to create delicious and healthy meals. Food may be donated from allotments, food banks, restaurants, cafes, food photographers, events and functions.

Ann's holiday project was a great short-term success. Then, at a course run by Liverpool Diocese to help people discern their calling, Ann felt God calling her to serve. At first she felt this might be serving the communion elements, but quickly realized that her faith was calling her to serve people through using food waste to create good nutritious meals to feed people in Wigan.

Ann had been involved with Wigan Warriors Community Foundation and through them discovered some possible premises for a cafe. She got a cafe up and running in two weeks. In the first 12 months the cafe has used 60 tonnes of food, which otherwise would have become food waste, to feed 22,000 people. It is open to anyone, and people can pay in money or in kind. The cafe is not aimed at any one section of the community but is very much for anybody who wants to come in and be fed.

Ann has done all this in her 'spare time'. Although the cafe now has three employees, most of the staff are volunteers. They work closely with Wigan Council and various other local organizations.

Ann's vision, inspired by her love and care for people, is a great illustration of the 'love–relate–create principles' in this book. She is now working on the 'create' opportunities for people to connect with Jesus as a community begins to form around the cafe. The diocese have asked Ann to become a Local Mission Leader as she begins the next part of this great story about what one person can do with vision, love and passion.

7

Telling the Jesus story

What are we trying to achieve through the new communities we are developing? I wonder if the first words of Mark's Gospel might help. He starts his Gospel by writing, 'The beginning of the good news of Jesus Christ' (Mark 1.1). I wonder if this is one way of summarizing your aim. We are trying to form communities that begin to reflect, show and tell the good news of Jesus. This good news brings transformation to people and communities as it does its work.

At the heart of telling the story of our faith is that it is good news! Telling the story of our faith, often called 'evangelism', is not very popular in our culture or even in the Church. It can seem more like bad news, with its unhealthy associations with intolerance, guilt, condemnation and manipulation. The term 'evangelism' was coined in the seventeenth century but it has its origins in the Greek term *euangelion*, which is translated in the Bible as 'good news' or 'gospel'.

At the time of Jesus, the Greek word was associated with the idea of celebration and spontaneous festivities. It was used to describe the huge celebrations to mark the Emperor's

birthday or the return of a victorious army. More personally it was applied to parents joyfully announcing the birth
of a child to their friends and neighbours. Behind the word
is the idea of party, celebration, festivity and the outpouring
of excitement and thanks.

Do we understand telling the story about Jesus in this way?
Is it for us a spontaneous celebration of what Jesus has done
and is doing? Is it the natural overflowing of our present
experience of Jesus and his good news to us?

It is important to remember that people do want to hear this
good news. A few years ago I found myself in a steam room.
I was relaxing alone, enjoying a few precious moments for
myself. A young man of about 30 entered the steam room. I
hoped he would not want to chat and I avoided eye contact.
But I was disappointed as immediately he began talking to
me. I soon discovered that he had his own successful business selling vinyl records. He then asked me what I did. I
considered making something up but then decided as a
church minister I should probably tell the truth. I thought
my revelation would close the conversation down. But it
had exactly the opposite effect. He quickly started telling
me that he was very successful but felt that there must be
more to life than making money. He felt very disillusioned
and was wondering what the real point of life was. What
followed was a fascinating conversation about the meaning
of life, and I talked freely about my own story of discovering
Jesus and his story for my life. At the end of the conversation, when I was nearly fainting from having been in the

steam room too long, he thanked me for the conversation. Then he said to me, 'I have tried to talk about this with my friends but they didn't want to and so I didn't know where to go with this.'

This experience made me ask how many people in our communities want to talk about spiritual questions. People are wanting to discover if there is good news available to them. The problem is they don't know who to talk to! If only we could establish thousands of small communities that made the good news accessible to people. Accessible to them in their neighbourhoods, workplaces, schools, colleges and social spaces.

It is vital to understand that telling the story of Jesus is not disconnected from the rest of the life of the community. This has been one of the great problems of the Church. Telling this good news has somehow got separated from the rest of the Christian life. But, like any good news, it is a natural overflowing of our present experience of something happening. It is not a special activity for a few people or a particular interest group for 'those types of people'. Like all those good news parts in our lives, like the birth of a child, getting a promotion, or our new car, we can't keep quiet about it. You only have to look at Facebook, Twitter or Instagram to see this is true. We love celebrating and sharing good news.

It's also important to note that the good news is about Jesus. Its focus is on him, but he is also the agent of it. We are called to tell it in numerous ways, but ultimately it is his good news. We cannot force, coerce or even argue people into our communities; we tell the story and then let Jesus do his work in the lives of people. We need to understand that he takes the initiative in this work. We cannot make anyone a follower of Jesus; our role is to point the way and leave the impact to God. That is why prayer is so important, because this is ultimately a spiritual not a human activity.

Telling the good news

There are three elements that are crucial to telling the good news, and the elements need to be held together.

1 **Developing attractive community**
   This not an individualistic endeavour. The role of an attractive community is vital in telling the story. It is the place where people can see the good news being worked out in and through relationships, through how the community runs itself and how it works out conflict. The reality of how the message is embodied is crucial to the authenticity of the message. People get to see up close how the values of this good news operate for a group of people.

   This is where practices of social action operate as we live out God's mission. This is where compassion, peace, justice are lived out by the new community as they seek to bring transformation to the people and places around them.

But it's in the community we also do the work of under-standing what we believe. As people grow in their understanding of faith they are enabled to articulate it in the safety of the community. This happens both formally and informally: through specific opportunities to learn, but also through hanging out with others who are exploring their faith. We start to imbibe the story, which prepares us for the next step of translating this story so that others outside the community begin to explore it for themselves.

2   Enabling people to experience God

The Christian faith is not an exam. It is not simply a fixed form of information that we need cognitively to under-stand. It's not even only a stated set of beliefs that we agree to. We discovered in Huddersfield that people do not only want to find out information, they also want to experience transformation in their lives through directly experiencing God.

This can happen in a myriad of ways. Prayer is one of the best ways to link people directly to God. This can be done by using formal prayers or inviting people to pray their own words. It might consist of praying for people who are struggling in some part of their lives.

I know of one new community that uses silence very suc-cessfully. They meet on a Thursday morning and most of them are young mothers. Part of the morning is about 15–20 minutes of silence. The preschool children are looked after by other community members. With young children the opportunity for silence is very golden. But the aim of this silence is to discover what God might be saying through this time. So after the silence people are asked to share what they thought God might be saying. I need to stress that most of these people do not have church backgrounds and would not even consider themselves followers of Jesus yet.

Initially the leaders of the new community were worried about what might be said by the group members. It meant taking a risk, but they reported that it has always been an amazing time. They have never had to intervene and say that something was not helpful or just plain crazy! The people attending were regularly experiencing God, who they were discovering was alive and active.

Another great way people experience God is through worship. Again, this can happen in many ways depending on the community. It might revolve around the classic celebrations of Easter and Christmas. It can be large scale or simply three or four people. It can involve music and the arts to help engage with God. It might be all age, adult only or children only.

It is important to give space in worship for people to respond to God. In Huddersfield we used some classic spiritual practices and activities such as lighting candles or anointing with oil. We also discovered that Holy Communion and Agape meals were really important for people. These are great worship events which enable people not only to watch but also to take part. Through this we found that people experienced God in a way that was very deep for them.

3 **Using words that explain**

People often use the quote, 'Preach the gospel, use words if necessary.' This quote has been attributed to Francis of Assisi, but there is no evidence to confirm this. Ironically, Francis was part of a preaching order.

Our culture can be suspicious of words, which is sometimes reflected in the Church too. But words are part of telling the good news. Jesus used them, as did his first disciples. This does not mean we have long and boring monologues, but it does require space for explaining in words the experiences of God. Words help us to understand what is going on with God in our community and world.

The Day of Pentecost is a great example of how these three elements of community, experience and words can come together in telling the story of faith. In Acts 2, Luke makes clear that the disciples were 'together in one place'. They were developing the new community that was started by Jesus. But then comes this amazing experience of God through a violent wind and what seemed like tongues of fire. Whatever we might make of this experience, it certainly attracted a crowd who were astonished at what was going on. They were prompted to ask questions about what was happening. Luke tells us they were asking about the meaning of this experience.

This is where words come in. Peter gets up in front of them and explains what is happening. He makes it clear they are not drunk but explains to them what is happening and how it relates to the story of Jesus.

At Pentecost we see community, experience and words working together. The danger of only concentrating on community is that a new community can easily become like any other social group in a locality. Only focusing on experience can initially put people off from joining the group or leave confusion at what is happening. If the community only uses words, the group can seem very cerebral and divorced from the realities of life. Without any one of these elements the community can be unbalanced in telling the story. The three elements belong to each other and create a synergy that gives each element an increasing energy. Telling the story cannot be divorced or distanced from the nature of the community we are forming or the experiences of God we are encountering.

So what does this mean for a developing new community?

The importance of prayer

Prayer draws us into God and then he sends us into his world. Prayer also reminds us that the results of telling the story are God's work. It is worth considering how the community can be intentional in praying for both those who are telling the story and those hearing it. Where and how might this happen?

Know and practise your story of faith

In Huddersfield we realized it might help people to give them some basic training in telling their story. We found some possible courses and chose one that we felt was appropriate for our community. But it also meant we gave people opportunities to tell their story within the community. We decided if we couldn't tell each other our story how would we ever tell it to those outside the community? Most weeks during our worship we gave space for people to talk about how they were experiencing God now in their lives.

Leaders need to take the lead

It is very important that the leaders of the community model telling their story. This is vital if it is to be considered normal within the community. But it's also important that the leaders share not only their success but also where things didn't go so well. This gives people permission to try things out but stops unrealistic expectations. It also helps to show that we are all learners in this area.

Consider creative places for words that explain

Within the life of your community, where are the places of explanation? This might be through small study groups that look at a variety of topics or particular Gospel passages. Or it could be through explanation as part of your worship gatherings. In what creative ways might this happen to allow both teaching and discussion? My experience of working with those outside the Church is that they do want to hear about what we believe. They are suspicious if we are not honest about what we believe. But what they really want is space to explore, discuss and disagree with what they have heard. We found another great way of explaining faith was getting people with certain stories to tell them as part of an interview and then to give those listening an opportunity to ask questions of the speaker.

Telling the story is vital in the life of any community centred on Jesus. This story is good news and as we tell it we carry on the principles Jesus began in his first community 2,000 years ago.

The key things to remember

- We are trying to form communities that begin to reflect, show and tell the good news of Jesus.

- People are wanting to discover if there is good news available to them. The problem is they don't know who to talk to!

- It is vital to understand that telling the story of Jesus is not disconnected from the rest of the life of the community.

- We cannot make anyone a follower of Jesus; our role is to point the way and leave the impact to God.

- This not an individualistic endeavour, but the role of an attractive community is vital in telling the story.

- Words help us to understand what is going on with God in our community.

- Telling the story cannot be divorced or distanced from the nature of the community we are forming or the experiences of God we are encountering.

- Prayer draws us into God and then he sends us into his world.

Some important questions to consider

- Do you feel as individuals and as a community that this story of faith is good news?

- How is the 'good news' breaking out in your community?

- How is telling the story connected to community and experience in your community?

- In what ways are people experiencing God in your community? What is the impact of this?

- What part do words of explanation play in your community?

- How are leaders modelling the sharing of stories?

8

Growing disciples in community

The issue of growing disciples in community follows naturally from Chapter 6 on developing community. Those last words of Jesus in Matthew's Gospel remind us that our aim as a community is to grow disciples of Jesus, not just disciples. This is not primarily about external conformity, correct beliefs, attendance at meetings or events, but it is about Jesus. It's about how, with others, you follow, love, learn from and obey him. The slight problem is that you cannot see or physically follow. But millions of people have discovered they have become captivated by this person.

The word 'disciple' has a rich background in the ancient world. It was applied to an apprentice who was learning a skill from an expert in tasks as diverse as dancing, wrestling, music, hunting and writing. But it came to mean more than learning a skill or gaining an education, it also meant being committed to the person who was teaching you. It was the recognition that this relationship was key to learning. It was about being with the master and learning the master's practices and living them out.

The goal in all this is simply to become more like Jesus himself. Paul talks in his writings of Jesus being formed in us (Galatians 4.19) and that we are being transformed into his image (2 Corinthians 3.18). The words used here suggest that this is not just about us trying hard to follow Jesus but is really about what God is doing in us through his Holy Spirit. This doesn't mean we become perfect now, but it does mean that we are learning to live in the way he did in all that we do and are.

As Dallas Willard suggests in *Knowing Christ Today* (HarperOne, 2009), there are two key questions that we need to ask in thinking about growing disciples:

1 What kind of people as followers of Jesus are we meant to be?
2 What type of community is capable of developing that kind of people?

So what kind of people are we meant to be, not just when we are in 'religious mode' but in living out fully a human life? I was surprised to discover recently that the word 'disciple' is only used in the four Gospels and a few times in the Acts of the Apostles. It is not used in the rest of the New Testament, not even in letters written by Jesus' disciples. That seems surprising. Scholars have suggested that the word became associated with physically following Jesus around. The early churches thus grappled with how you can follow Jesus when you can't literally follow him. They therefore changed their wording and stopped using the word 'disciple'.

The words Paul often substitutes for disciple are 'with Christ' or 'in Christ'. He uses these terms 163 times to suggest what following Jesus might look like when you can't physically see Jesus now. For Paul, the kind of people we are meant to be is now inextricably linked to having a new identity in and through the risen Jesus.

At the beginning of his letter to the small church in Ephesus (Ephesians 1.3–14) he clearly tells these new followers of Jesus who they really are with or in Jesus. They were chosen to become children of God, with all the advantages of now being part of a royal family. They have experienced God's grace, experiencing his unconditional love for them as his children. They are totally forgiven people who are therefore free from their past. God has enabled them to understand what he is doing in this world through Jesus and they have received a new life which starts now and leads into eternity. God has moved into their lives through his Spirit, to give them the strength and abilities to live out this life. And finally these things are not just for their own benefit but are part of God's amazing plans for a new heaven and a new earth.

These first few words in Paul's letter were not put there to get on the right side of his readers through flattery, but to remind them who they really are and who their true identity is in the face of the Empire of Rome, which would be telling them a very different tale. Paul was saying to them, 'This is who you really are right now through Jesus, this is your true identity. Now live out this new identity and stop being who you are not.' As a friend said to me recently, 'God sees in us what we don't see in ourselves till we do.' Discipleship is about seeing in ourselves what God already sees in us. It is realizing that our past does not determine our present, but what defines us as humans is Jesus' identity which is being formed in us.

Paul's so-called 'ethical teaching' in his letters is really about how you then live out this new life if you are children of God, loved totally and forgiven completely! It is identity leading to action.

So what kind of community do we need to be to enable us all to discover our true identity in Jesus? It is worth noting that growing disciples is not an individualistic activity. Nearly all the use of the word 'disciple' in the Gospels is in the plural form. Paul's letters are almost always addressed not to individuals but these new developing Christian communities. Discovering our true identity as human beings and living it out happens in the context of community.

Here are some principles to help you reflect on what kind of community you might need to develop to grow disciples of Jesus.

1 **We are all full-time students of Jesus.**
   We need to realize that the school for disciples is always in operation. Every moment is an opportunity to learn more about God, about ourselves and others, about our community and God's world. Often Jesus' disciples

learnt key lessons with Jesus on the way to places. This doesn't just happen in formal times of learning, in a Bible study or discussion group. But it happens informally at any point in our day. So it's really important to allow time for intentional reflection on our own and with others, to ask the simple questions, 'What is God teaching me today about who he is and who I am?' 'Where are the places, who are the people, what are the situations where God is teaching me?' Reflection on our daily lives is a key spiritual discipline. We can begin to discern where we are discovering God's blessing each day, where we might feel isolated or in the wilderness, what the day's battles looked like and where we experienced defeat or victory.

2 **The biggest enemy of discovering who we really are is hurry.**
The 'unexamined life is not worth living', are words attributed to Socrates that remind us how important reflection is. The pace at which we live our lives can easily mean we miss the work of God's action in our lives. The unrelenting busyness of our lives means we end up not living life but skimming over it. This is why community is really important in helping us to stop and reflect.

3 **Community helps us to construct life-giving rhythms.**
It is very difficult to find good rhythms on our own. Coming together with others helps us to do this. The basic rhythm in Scripture is the Sabbath principle; the one day in seven to worship, celebrate and reflect upon

God. We are told that God rested on the seventh day. What does this mean? That he ceased all his activity? No, I think it has more the sense of completeness, of God having done all that was needed and that he is in control of his creation. Our Sabbath is about us admitting we are not in control but we come to serve the one who is. It doesn't all count on us, so we can truly rest and reflect because God is in control, the King is on the throne.

The situations and contexts of people's lives may require some flexibility and creativity in forming a community rhythm. But it is important to work out together what this might look like.

4 **We need each other.**
Community is about understanding that we are both fellow students and teachers. We are on this spiritual journey together, but we can also learn from each other. Paul sums this up when he writes to a church, 'join in imitating me, and observe those who live according to the example you have in us' (Philippians 3.17). Coming together means that we benefit from others' experiences and insights, and so we all grow.

But community is where we also practise the new life. It's easier to talk about love than to love those around us. Community gives us the space for a practice court, where we can try out the qualities of living our new identity. In the New Testament there are over 50 instances of 'one another'. These include commands to love one another, accept one another, bear with one another, be hospitable with one another, forgive one another and be kind to one another. It's in doing these actions that we truly learn about ourselves. Our learning comes out of living out our new identities with each other. It's much easier to understand the notion of forgiveness than to actually forgive someone in the community who has wronged us.

5 **Understand the balance of failure, effort and grace.**
These three elements make a very powerful tool for our growth as disciples. Paul sums up the constructive tension that exists between them when he writes, 'Not that I have already obtained this or have already reached the goal; but I press on to make it my own, because Christ Jesus has made me his own' (Philippians 3.12).

Part of our development is in understanding that we are not fully who we are meant to be. This reminds us to be humble and honest people. But the danger of awareness of our shortcomings is that we feel like giving up. What's the point of going on, we ask, when we keep making the same mistakes over and over again? Our weak spots continually let us down and make us despondent. But Paul uses very strong language about the discipline of keeping going. This doesn't just happen, but requires effort and work on our part. We do need to put the work in, Paul says.

This can easily lead to thinking that being a disciple is all about trying harder and doing more. This can be a very depressing human-centred approach. But Paul reminds us of the importance of grace. In the face of our own failure and efforts we are held by Jesus, and he is never going to let go. We are already new people in Jesus, already loved, forgiven and blessed.

In our approach as individuals, and especially in the life of the community, we need to make sure we keep the tension of these three elements in their correct balance. We need all three for healthy, growing community.

6 **Discover the activities we can do that enable us to become more of who we truly are.**

God has given activities by which we become more like Jesus and more of our true selves. We see these practices throughout Scripture and the history of the Church. These include prayer, reading Scripture, worship, service, confession, silence, fasting, sacrifice and fellowship. These seem to be the disciplines where, over thousands of years, people have met with God and others and discovered transformation in their lives. It is important to understand that it is through these practices that we discover more of God and experience more of his life in our lives, as individuals and as a community.

7 **This sends us out.**

There are two key movements we see in operation in the Bible. One is moving closer to God and the other is being sent out by God to be a blessing to others. Both are fundamental to our lives and the two movements are interrelated. It is important to understand that growing as disciples is also related to serving others and being involved in God's mission. As we discover more about God and the identity we have in Jesus, the overflow of this is seen in our serving others from the gratefulness of our own experiences. We cannot keep this to ourselves and it needs to cascade out to others and often to those on the margins of society. This is not purely inward growth, which is solely concerned with how I am doing, some kind of selfish self-fulfilment. It is about being transformed by God as we are called into his work of bringing transformation to his world.

How you use these disciple principles as you continue to construct your community will depend on your own specific context. There are lots of ways of combining these together to create something that is creative, attractive and God-invigorating. But the basis of all this will be seen in the following.

1 **Tell: 'Do it like this.'**

As I have said before, there is a place for teaching. In learning any new thing you need to know the rules and exercise them properly. In John's Gospel Jesus makes a clear connection between love and obedience. For example, he says, 'Those who love me will keep my word' (John 14.23). We tend to drive a wedge between love and instruction, but Jesus makes clear there is a strong link. Jesus wants to tell us about how to live the new life of identity in him. There are lots of way of doing this, but instruction is important.

2 Show: 'Do it like this.'

To learn, we need not only to be told how to do something but shown how to do it. We learn by doing what someone else is doing. Paul writes to the church in Thessalonica, 'And you became imitators of us and of the Lord' (1 Thessalonians 1.6). We learn in community by seeing how others do things and beginning to imitate them. We can all learn from each other as we see faith worked out in and through the community.

3 Participate: 'Do it like this.'

In the end we learn in the doing. God invites us as a community to participate in discovering his life in our lives. It's important that people understand this is an invitation for everyone. Disciples are not the experts or the most experienced – they are all who journey in and with Jesus.

Finally it is worth noting that though the word I have used throughout this book is 'community', we are really talking about church. Church not in a particular idealized form, but as a developing community of disciples. Church is not primarily a set of practices that we do but ultimately a set of four relationships. First, it is all about how we relate to God and how he relates to us. Second, it is about how we relate to each other as we live out this new identity in Jesus. Third, this new identity sends us out into God's world to relate to it and serve God's purposes in it. Finally, we are in relationship to the history and tradition of which we are a part. (For more about what church is, see Michael Moynagh, *Church for Every Context*, SCM Press, 2012, ch. 5)

The practices of the community – worship, prayer, service and so on – exist to serve these four relationships, not vice versa. We need continually to ask how what we are doing is enabling us to discover our real identity in God, through relating to each other, to God's world and to our tradition.

The key things to remember

- Discipleship is not primarily about external conformity, correct beliefs, attendance at meetings and events, but it is about Jesus.

- Being a disciple was about being with the master, learning the master's practices and living them out.

- The words Paul seems to substitute for 'disciple' are 'with Christ' or 'in Christ'.

- 'God sees in us what we don't see in ourselves till we do.'

- Discovering our true identity as human beings and living it out happens in the context of community.

- Every moment is an opportunity to learn more about God, about ourselves and others, about our community and God's world.

- The unrelenting busyness of our lives means we end up not living life but skimming over it.

- Community is about understanding we are both fellow students and teachers.

- In the face of our own failure and efforts we are held by Jesus and he is never going to let go.

Some important questions to consider

- How do you understand this idea of a new identity in Jesus?

- What kinds of rhythms are beginning to operate in your community?

- How are you balancing the elements of failure, effort and grace in your community?

- Can you identify the elements of tell, show and participate in your community?

Case study
Fun-Key Church, Richmond,
North Yorkshire

Some leaders discover they start something new by accident. Gillian, mum of three boys, never set out to start a church or to be involved in such things. She never considered herself a leader, had never even thought of doing a reading in church! Her husband is a lay reader and she has always seen her main role as supporting him. They are part of a traditional congregation where, like many other churches, there are few younger people or children.

Events changed things for Gillian. Her husband had a bicycle accident which meant she went to a diocesan event instead of him. The event was about connecting with younger families. She went to the meeting thinking she was only going to report back to her husband and the church. Following that meeting, a one-off Exploring Easter event was held with 75 people attending. This helped Gillian realize: we can do something in our church for younger families. We can connect with many new people. When she was told by someone they couldn't really do anything in the church building, she thought, 'O yes, we can.' This led to some big changes for Gillian.

With the support of her vicar, she recruited a small team and they started Fun-Key Church. They used the church building, as there are no other suitable facilities available. Its tag line is 'fun, faith and fellowship for all ages'. It encourages families, friends and individuals with none or some church experience to worship with the theme of the day aided by craft, music, activities and a warm atmosphere and no charge. Worship is built around a series of zones and part of its strength is its simplicity.

Fun-Key has been meeting monthly for the last four years in the local church building. It is continuing to evolve as it seeks to connect with new people. Usual attendance is between 50 and 70. The average age of adults is around 40 years younger than the traditional Sunday congregation. You can find out more about Fun-Key at https://funkeychurchatstmarysrichmond.wordpress. com/about/.

9

How to avoid rotas and other useful advice

I saw a book last week which argued that the pace of life in the western world was getting faster all the time. It certainly feels like that in my life. The promise of time-saving gadgets only means we now try to fit even more into our hectic lives. I wonder how many plates you feel you are spinning presently in your life? They might be the plates of career, home, family responsibilities, keeping fit, friendships, or many other things. It is exhausting keeping all the plates in the air with the fear that we can't really cope. And now you are thinking about starting or helping to develop this new community. Probably you will be doing this in your spare time and there isn't much of that to go round. So what do you do about it? How do you find the time to do this? How do you ensure that you do not burn yourself out? How can you ensure that this experience of creating new Christian community is life-enhancing and not life-draining? What is a proper sustainable pace for your community that brings you closer to God and each other?

Here are seven simple steps for you and your community.

1 **Don't think balance.**

   You might be surprised by this one! I often hear leaders say, 'You need to lead a balanced life.' By 'balance' what they mean is you try to live in such a way that equal attention and focus is given to all the parts of your life. This well-meaning advice is either impossible or it makes life very bland and lacklustre. I have given up filling in various timetables to check whether I am leading a balanced lifestyle. They are a waste of time and make me feel stressed simply filling them in.

2 **Find the right rhythms.**

   In reality we don't live by balance but by rhythms. We see this in things like the seasons, night and day, and the week and weekend. The whole way God has designed the world and our lives is around sustainable rhythms.

   The issue for us and our communities is to discover the right rhythms. Rhythms are about building in sustainable patterns of intensity and rest.

3 **Identify peak moments.**

   You therefore need to consider when your peak moments are as a community and understand these might be busy times. So you then need to find other times to rest and recreate. You could use the classic church seasons to create these peak moments including Advent/Christmas, Lent/Easter and Pentecost. Or you could use other moments in the year, such as schools and colleges starting the academic year, the New Year and its promise of new resolutions, the holiday season of the summer, or maybe national or local holidays or celebrations. These are the moments and special times around which you can build specific activities. These will be intense times for the community for meeting with God and each other. In Huddersfield we identified these key times as Christmas and New Year, the summer holidays for various activities we ran, and the autumn, which is a great time for cultivating spiritual growth and development.

4   **Recognize your own community seasons.**
These seasons will exist, and it is good to work with them and relate your peak moments to them. In Huddersfield we pinpointed these moments from our observations of how people lived their lives in our local communities. They will differ from community to community, depending on your context, but these were ours.

- **Start-up season**
  This was basically September to Christmas. With young adults and families this was very much the season for everything starting up. It was the start of the academic year, but lots of other activities for people including clubs and social events started again after the summer. This seemed to be a season of energy. Even though there were lots of other activities going on in people's lives, this was the best time to have specific mission and training activities. There

was a number of specific short courses and groups going on.

- **Growth season**

  From Christmas to Easter was growth season. This seemed to mirror the coming of spring. Again, there was a lot of energy around. We would often find this was the best time for helping those from outside the Church to discover more about Jesus. We would run our Just Looking group, which was a simple way for people to explore more about Jesus by reading parts of Luke's Gospel together. It was also a good season for people wanting to grow in and develop their faith. This happened through specific small-group discipleship activities helping people think through how Jesus related to every aspect of their lives.

- **Consolidation season**

  This small window between Easter and June always felt it had less energy connected with it. It reflected being between growth and regroup seasons. This wasn't the time to start new things but was a good season to build on what people had been learning from the start-up and growth seasons. This was a great period for developing one-to-one mentoring times for people, or extra time for some of the groups from the growth season.

- **Regroup season**

  Summer was the time for rest and recreation for individuals and the community. Our normal weekly corporate worship activity was paired down to the minimum, meeting together very simply to eat and worship together. Most of our small-group activities and service activities ceased during this period. It was a great period, though, for social activities for the community – lots of time for parties and celebrations. Jesus had such times for himself and his disciples. He said to his disciples on one occasion, 'Come away to a deserted place all by yourselves and rest a while' (Mark 6.31).

5 **Understand that rhythms change.**

   Rhythms exist to serve the community not vice versa. So you need continually to ask if these rhythms are still suitable for you. I received an email this morning from a community who are changing the way they meet corporately because they have understood that their rhythms are changing. Having started as a community of young adults they are finding that the advent of young children is making them rethink how they meet together.

6 **Practise gratitude and generosity.**

   This is really important in any season. Make sure you are the kind of community where appreciation is given and received. In what ways can you show gratitude to people for what they are doing, and how can you become a generous community? It is easy to quickly take people for granted. These vital gospel attributes often need to start with the leaders setting the relational tone for the community.

7 **Don't lose your focus in any season.**
Remind yourselves regularly in the different seasons why you are developing a new community. I discovered this was key in the life of the community. I tried to find different ways in the varying seasons to say to the community that we started this for the majority of the people in our town who are presently unconnected to any church. We wanted them to be able to connect and reconnect with Jesus. This is key to the community's motivation as it develops. Our role as leaders was to work out what this motivation looked like in the particular seasons.

You may have noticed in these seven steps that I have not mentioned rotas yet! You may need them or you may not, depending on the size and type of community you have. But the seasons and rhythms do play havoc with them. In the right place and at the right time they are very useful. But there might be a season for organization and a season not to be organized!

Most of these steps relate to the whole community, but there are some important issues to consider for the leaders of a new community. They are often related to the particular pressures of starting something new. Leaders need to ensure that a number of things are in place for their own health and viability.

1 **Inputs need to match outputs.**

 You are giving out all the time, but where are you receiving back? This is particularly important for your own spiritual life. Running on empty for very long is not good. Where are the places of input for you within the community?

2 **Give priority to your own discipleship.**

 Remember you are a disciple of Jesus too. You need to make sure your leadership work does not negate the work of God in you. It is important that you find your identity in Jesus not in the success or otherwise of this new community. You are not what you lead.

3 **You need others.**

 This is a vital area for your health. You need other people who can give you wise counsel, advice and support. Do you have a person or people like this? If not, where might you find such people? Your denomination or a local church might be able to help you find a suitable person. Different words are used for such people – accompanier, coach, consultant or mentor. But they are really important. I have found such people to be vital during my own life. They have encouraged me and saved me from making some serious and costly mistakes.

 As well as an accompanier you also need people to whom you are accountable as a leader. This may be someone from your local church or denomination. This is not about someone checking up on you. It's important that in a positive way there are people holding you to account for what is happening. They are vital in giving you support and asking you key questions about the new community. They are critical friends who play a vital role in keeping you and the community on track. If you do not have a person like this it is important that you quickly find someone.

But as well as such roles your friends are really important. Don't allow yourself to become isolated. You need friends to laugh with, play with, have fun with and learn with.

Hopefully you will not require these suggestions, but here are some possible danger signs for leaders who need to get back to a life-giving rhythm.

- **Motivation has gone.** You have lost the sense of why you are doing what you are doing.

- **Emotional numbness.** There are inevitably highs and lows in any leadership role. The danger comes when you feel nothing about what is happening.

- **People drain you.** You find being around those in the community brings you down.

- **Little things make you disproportionately angry.** Woe betide if anyone is two minutes late for a meeting.

- **You find yourself becoming cynical.**

- **You don't laugh any more.** Not everything about leading is fun but there should be times to laugh together and enjoy what you are doing.

Finding the right rhythm for yourselves and the community is vital. I can't tell you what will work for you as it depends on your particular context, but I can tell you that finding it is imperative. This will need some experimentation, but the principles in this chapter will hopefully mean you flourish rather than flounder.

The key things to remember

- In reality we don't live by balance but by rhythms.

- Rhythms are about building in sustainable patterns of intensity and rest.

- Rhythms exist to serve the community not vice versa. So you need to continually ask whether the rhythms you have are still suitable for you.

- Make sure you are the kind of community where appreciation is given and received.

- Remind yourselves regularly in the different seasons why you are involved in your project.

- Running on empty for very long is not good.

- You need other people who can give you wise counsel, advice and support.

- The role of friends is really important. Don't allow yourself to become isolated.

Some important questions to consider

- What rhythms are you beginning to discover for your community?

- Are there discernible seasons in your community?

- How can you respond to these seasons through the activities of the community?

- What kind of regrouping time does the community experience?

- As leaders, are your outputs matched by your input?

- What advice and support are you receiving as leaders?

Case study
Pebbles, St Lawrence, Essex

You are never too old to start something new. Retired couple Clive and Lesley, who had been involved in children's and youth work for many years, wanted to encourage young families in their small village in Essex. The village has about 800 residents. Their church really shared this desire but the problem was they never came on a Sunday.

So Clive and Lesley decided to do something about it. They started something they called Pebbles, which meets in the church hall. It meets on a Monday morning for two hours and is aimed at mothers and carers and under-fives, although sometimes fathers or grandparents attend. It is a mixture of a warm-hearted community and a Christian celebration with prayers, songs and Bible readings. Much of the content is aimed at the adults to help them develop a living faith. Clive and Lesley are much older than those attending but they have a 'grandparently' role to this fledgling community. Pebbles always starts with tea and coffee and lots of time to chat and catch up. Prayer is usually offered and gratefully received. The budget is very low. The only cost is for the drinks!

Often they have around 40 people attending, with about 20 adults. At holiday times older siblings also attend. None of these people come to the Sunday congregation but they have found their church on a Monday at 10 a.m.

10

Ending and beginnings

Life often revolves around beginnings and endings. You have made it to the end of this book – well done. This, though, may now be the beginning of something exciting as you step out in action. This might be the point of moving from theory to action. Maybe this is the moment for you to answer God's call and begin something new. To do that might even involve ending something else.

You are not alone in this position. Let me encourage you by telling you that you are part of a quiet revolution that is happening right now. In many places and churches, often driven by a variety of circumstances, people are asking fundamental questions about the nature of faith and church. Thousands of people are dreaming of a different way to do and be church to connect with the majority of people who are not part of church presently. Many of these people are not recognized church leaders but so-called 'ordinary people'. Like the people I mentioned in Chapter 1, they are asking the right questions about how they connect people around them with God. They are wondering what might be possible and whether there might be a different way forward for the Church.

We are all trying to find our way to know how to respond to these questions. We are all trying to edge forwards, learning from experience and experimentation. You will not know all the answers at this stage but you hopefully have a sense of the direction and even shape of what might take place. So what do you require to respond, to move from questioning to action, to move from thinking to undertaking?

I would suggest that there are three key things you require:

1 **Some tested basic practices and principles that this book gives you**
   Have confidence in them because these principles have been tried and tested in many different situations. These will start you off in the right direction as you use them. They will give you a solid foundation which will help to produce a healthy new community. But remember, as I have constantly told you, these are principles and not a blueprint. You will have to do the critical work of discovering how these principles work out in your context. This is where the important work of listening, praying, talking and learning is so critical.

2 **Other people**
   It is important that you are doing this with other people. If you haven't got others around you then you need to find them quickly. You need a group or team to do this with. This is your immediate priority for prayer and action. Who has God put around you who might or could share your dreams and vision?

It is also good to meet with other like-minded people who are doing similar things. The resource list at the end of this chapter will give you some useful links. It may be that in your area your denomination is running events to bring people together. It would be worth following up links to see what is already happening. It might also be helpful to visit other communities that are beginning, to be inspired and to learn from them for your situation.

3 **Faith**

Remember that this is not a purely human endeavour – you are partnering with God in his mission. The key question to ask is, 'Do I really believe that God can use me in this?' It's important to appreciate that the word 'believe' in the Gospels does not mean an academic-type understanding. Much more it reflects a willingness to trust and act. It means that even with all your questions, doubts and fears you are willing to trust Jesus in this and give it a go! You may find that what seems like the end of a journey is only really the beginning of an amazing adventure. Do you trust enough to take that first step of adventure?

I am hoping that, as with Jill, Philip and Jen, James, Lillian, Michael and Juliet, whom we met in Chapter 1, the questions are likely to lead you into action. It is exciting to think where your dreams might lead you; to begin to imagine the transformation that you might witness in people's lives and in your community. I really hope you will continue on this adventure, to see what God might achieve through you. Remember, he can use you and he wants to use you. The ending is your beginning!

Resources

This list of resources would be beneficial at the stage of beginning a new community centred on Jesus. Most of these resources have a short commentary, so hopefully you can find what is most worthwhile. It would also be worth checking out the website for your local diocese, district or area, which will tell you about local people and resources that might be able to offer support and encouragement. Most of the major denominations and streams also have websites with resources that might be suitable for your situation.

Useful books to read

These books are selected to be most help at the beginning of starting something new.

Shane Claiborne, *The Irresistible Revolution: Living as an Ordinary Radical*, Grand Rapids, MI: Zondervan, 2006.
This is a great book about developing a faith community rooted in belief, action and love.

Vincent J. Donovan, *Christianity Rediscovered*, London: SCM Press, 2001.
This is an old book which is the story of a missionary discovering how to explain and live the gospel with the Masai people in Africa. There is so much to learn from this for our contemporary situation.

Michael Moynagh, *Being Church, Doing Life*, Oxford: Monarch Books, 2014.
A great book on how to start communities in the midst of ordinary life, packed with good examples.

Phil Potter, *Pioneering a New Future: A Guide to Shaping Change and Changing the Shape of Church*, Abingdon: BRF, 2015.
A great book on starting something new and how to cope with the changes it brings.

Alan Roxburgh, *Missional Map-Making: Skills for Leading in Times of Transition*, San Francisco, CA: Jossey-Bass, 2010.
A book for leaders on how to lead in mission and bring change.

Jean Vanier, *Community and Growth*, London: Darton, Longman & Todd, 1979.
Another older book, but with lots of wise counsel on how to develop realistic community, based on the author's experiences of the L'Arche communities.

Websites

The Church of England Pioneer website, www.cofepioneer.
org, has links to this book with further information,
resources and stories. You can also follow pioneering
developments on Twitter @CofEpioneering.

Fresh Expressions website, www.freshexpressions.org.uk, is
brimming with lots of stories, ideas and resources. A good
place to start to find more resources and information.

The Guide, www.freshexpressions.org.uk/guide, contains
how-to-do-it advice on starting, developing and sustaining
fresh expressions of church based on shared experiences. All
the material is based on listening to hundreds of different
stories on how fresh expressions begin and are sustained.

Three Minute Guides, www.freshexpressions.org.uk/guide/
essential, are seven three-minute downloadable guides on
starting fresh expressions.

New Way of Being Church, www.newway.org.uk/aboutus/,
supports small communities, embracing a diverse group of
people whose gifts and calling are directed to the well-being
of our local communities.

Urban Expression, www.urbanexpression.org.uk/, is a mission agency that recruits, equips, deploys and networks self-financing teams, pioneering creative and relevant expressions of the Christian Church in under-churched areas of the inner city.

Cafe Church, www.cafechurch.net, provides training and advice for those hoping to set up a cafe church.

Messy Church, www.messychurch.org.uk/, is a way of being church for families involving fun which helps people encounter Jesus as Lord and Saviour.

Rural Expression, www.ruralexpression.org.uk/drupal/, is a mission initiative that recruits, equips, deploys and networks self-financing teams, pioneering, creative and relevant expressions of the Christian Church among under-churched groups and communities in rural areas.

Church Army centres of mission
www.churcharmy.org.uk/Groups/233846/Church_Army/
Church_Army/Our_work/Centres_of_Mission/Centres_
of_Mission.aspx
New communities in specific areas in the UK.

Methodist Church Fresh Expressions
www.methodist.org.uk/mission/fresh-expressions

How to finance a fresh expression
www.parishresources.org.uk
A very helpful basic guide on finance.

Church Army Research Unit
www.churcharmy.org.uk/Groups/244926/Church_Army/
Church_Army/Our_work/Research/Research.aspx
Research on what is happening with and in fresh expressions of church, mainly in the Church of England.

Training resources

Mission Shaped Ministry (MSM)
www.missionshapedministry.org
MSM is an excellent one-year course which takes people on a learning journey as part of a supportive community, training them for ministry in fresh expressions of church. Usually the course consists of three Saturdays, eight evenings and a weekend but there are more flexible ways of using the material.

mission shaped intro (msi)
www.freshexpressions.org.uk/msi
msi helps people to reconnect with the communities they are called to serve and to re-imagine the forms of church that are needed for the twenty-first century. It takes you on a creative and reflective journey looking at the need for new ways of being church through six downloadable sessions.

ReSource Training
https://pioneer.cms-uk.org/pioneer-mission-leadership-training-course/resource-mission-weekends/
A series of immersive mission-experience weekends through which you meet people who are doing mission, hang out with their communities, hear their stories and then think about what you can learn for your own situation.

Crucible training course
www.urbanexpression.org.uk/training/crucible-course
Crucible consists of three intensive training weekends each year to equip Christians to follow Jesus on the margins by creating new communities.

CMS Pioneer Training
https://pioneer.cms-uk.org/pioneer-mission-leadership-training-course/course-details/
A modular course, which means it is very flexible.

CPL Pioneer School
www.centreforpioneerlearning.org.uk/index.php/pioneer-school.php
Pioneer School is a course specifically designed for those leading new communities. It is held on six Saturdays over a period of about eight months. Each day is structured, with input and discussion in the morning followed by small, peer-led groups in the afternoon.

Mentoring training

www.cpas.org.uk/church-resources/mentoring-matters/#.
Vx9C7032bIU

An easy-to-use pack with everything you need to start a
church-based mentoring network: identifying, equipping
and resourcing mentors.

Mentor Connect

www.mentorconnect.org.uk/find-a-mentor

Helps leaders to find a mentor.

Ugly Duckling Company

www.theuglyducklingcompany.com/

A number of excellent resources that attempt to create
spaces for people to explore some of the big and not-so-
big questions of life. A great source for developing spiritual
conversations.